Carved slab from Ballinvally, Co. Meath, Ireland.
Approximate width 52 ins (142 cm). Rubbed by
the author in the National Museum, Dublin.

Ancient Carvings
in Britain: A Mystery

Evan Hadingham

Ancient Carvings
in Britain: A Mystery

Garnstone Press

ANCIENT CARVINGS IN BRITAIN: A MYSTERY
is published by
THE GARNSTONE PRESS LIMITED
59 Brompton Road, London SW3 1DS
© Evan Hadingham, 1974
ISBN: 0.85511.391.X

Printed in Great Britain by
REDWOOD BURN LIMITED Trowbridge & Esher

Contents

1. View along the ruined passageway of a pre-historic tomb (Cairn I) at the cemetery of Lough-crew, Co. Meath, Ireland. The passage is aligned towards the largest tomb in the group, Cairn T, on the nearby ridge of Sliabh na Caillighe (The Hill of the Witch). The zig-zag carvings are typical of the dozens of decorated stones at this legendary site.

2. The Clear Island stone, Co. Cork, Ireland. Maximum width approximately 15 ins (38 cm).

Preface

Scattered over the moor-tops of northern England, Scotland and Ireland are hundreds of prehistoric carvings—strange apparently abstract curves, circles, branching lines and hollows—which have lain unnoticed for thousands of years and even today are ignored by all but the keen-eyed walker or archaeologist. In Ireland, the current excavations and restoration of the great tombs of the Boyne, with their massive ornamented stones covered with spirals, lozenges, zig-zags and arcs, have brought to public attention a remarkable tradition of prehistoric art in stone. Only recently has a small number of studies in academic journals begun to throw light on some of the extraordinary puzzles which the carvings present, questions related not only to the meaning of the patterns but also to the society which created them. This book is an attempt to introduce these problems to a general reader in an easily understood form, with full references to where the original papers and the carvings themselves may be found. It presents some of the abundant evidence that the meaning of these ancient signs and symbols cannot be resolved by a single theory or solution, despite the attempts of so many scholars and students, past and present, to impose one. There is a 'magical' or 'mystical' impulse which only our imagination can supply, and this transforms any interest in the carvings into something more than a dry and remote study.

The illustrations have been assembled over a number of years and there is no attempt to provide the uniformity appropriate to a scholarly work. However, the research and writing of the text could not have been undertaken without the extensive advice and criticism of many authorities, notably Dr Aubrey Burl, Miss M. Campbell, Miss F. Finlay, Mr R. W. B. Morris, Professor M. J. O'Kelly, Miss E. Shee, Professor A. Thom and others. I am also grateful to Ernest Black, David and Clarissa Keighley, Miss K. Lindsay-MacDougall, Patrick Oates, Jon and Frances Patrick, Mike and Georgess Roberts, Richard Turner, and Marian Youngblood, for their assistance with fieldwork and general questions.

The research facilities granted to me by Alnwick Castle Museum, Cork Museum, the National Museum of Ireland, Dublin, the National Museum of Antiquities of Scotland, Edinburgh, and by the Haddon Library, Cambridge, the University Library, Cambridge, the Society of Antiquaries Library, London, and the Institute of Archaeology Library, London, were invaluable. I wish to acknowledge the support of Educational Expeditions International, Boston, and its field expeditions to mid-Argyll under Dr G. S. Hawkins which permitted a close study of the carvings in this region.

I have deliberately avoided the question of the recalibration of radiocarbon dating in order to simplify the discussion. The specialist may note that all dates are given in uncorrected (b.c.) radiocarbon years and that the sources are Giot 1971, O'Kelly, M. J., 1969 and Shee 1972.

E. H.

1 The Art of the Great Tombs

Legend and History

For thousands of years a remarkable collection of prehistoric art lay buried under the rubble of huge burial mounds in the east of Ireland. Although the great carved slabs of the funerary passages and chambers were often concealed under tons of rock, the mounds themselves were not forgotten in the popular imagination. To the monks who laboriously transcribed the remains of ancient heroic cycles, or to the local teller of folk tales, names like Tara and Knowth meant the great centres of royal power in pagan times. The stories which were told to explain these mounds show how they were held in time-honoured veneration and even fear as the haunts of gods, heroes and giants. When Dean 1 Swift and Richard Sheridan visited the cemetery of cairns at Lough-crew, County Meath, dotted along a range of hills so prominent that it is possible to see from one coast of Ireland to another, they had little to guide their impressions except the tales of a local gardener, which it was reputed that Swift himself had versified. Loughcrew was the haunt of the huntress Gavorgue who . . .

> Determined now her tomb to build
> Her ample skirts with stones she filled
> And dropped a heap on Carnmore
> Then stepped one thousand yards, to Loar,
> And dropped another goodly heap;
> And then with one prodigious leap
> Gained Carnbeg; and on its height
> Displayed the wonders of her might.
> . . . And when approached death's awful doom
> Her chair was placed within the womb
> Of hills whose tops with heather bloom.

And there, by the side of the largest of the Loughcrew cairns, stood the Hag's Chair itself, a throne hewn out of a solid block of stone ten feet long and six feet high. What was the great heap of Newgrange, the 'white-topped brugh of the Boyne', if not the burying place of the powerful Uí Néill dynasties, or, according to another tradition, the house of the god Dagda Mór and his hero son the wandering Aonghus?

The fertile ridge enclosed by a curling loop of the River Boyne, about 28 miles from Dublin, continued to be an important centre even into historic times. A poet, writing of it sometime before the tenth century when the maintenance of routes was part of kingly duty, says 'Wide thy road with traffic of hundreds, O lucent land of grass and

3

Side numbers refer to 'Notes On The Text'—page 105.

3. Map of some important sites mentioned in this book.

4. The Hag's Chair, Lough-crew, a massive carved stone in the kerb ring around the base of Cairn T.

NOTE
Scale in inches shown in some photographs.

wagons!' The historical annals tell us that the prehistoric mound of Knowth was the seat of the northern Brega and their greatest king, Congalach, who nearly succeeded in imposing his overlordship over all Ireland in the turbulent mid-tenth century. Archaeologists have recently confirmed that an important defended settlement had existed on top of the mound as far back as the Early Christian period. The bend of the Boyne is densely covered with unexplored forts, prehistoric ritual monuments and earthworks which are still being discovered on aerial photographs and which could belong to many periods. The continuity of traditions at other places such as Tara, about 10 miles south of the Boyne, is equally evident from the written sources. At Tara, Muirchú, the seventh century biographer of Patrick, set the saint's greatest struggle with the powers of paganism wielded by the Druids of king Lóegaire. The overlords of the Uí Néill were inaugurated on a prehistoric mound that was already 3,000 years old at the time of Patrick's visit.

But who originally built these monuments? When the famous

5

antiquary Edward Lhwyd came to Newgrange in 1699, shortly after the rediscovery of the burial chamber, he made a shrewd guess based partly on the 'carving and rude sculpture' which he had seen inside the tomb. 'It should follow' he wrote, 'that it was some place of sacrifice or burial 2 of the ancient Irish'. After some of the rubble had been removed from the mound by the landowner,

> 'a very broad flat stone' was exposed, '. . . placed edgewise at the bottom of the mount. This they discovered to be the door of a cave, which had a long entry leading to it. At the first entering we were forced to creep; but still as we went on, the pillars on each side of us were higher and higher; and coming into the cave we found it about 20 foot high. In this cave, on each hand of us was a cell or apartment, and another went straight forward opposite to the entry. In those on each hand was a very broad shallow bason of stone, situated at the edge. The bason in the right hand apartment stood in another; that on the left was single, and in the apartment straight forward there was none at all . . . The great pillars round this cave, supporting the mount, were not at all hewn or wrought; but were such rude stones as those of Abury in Wiltshire, and rather more rude than those of Stonehenge; but those about the basons, and some elsewhere, had such barbarous sculpture (viz. spiral like a snake, but without distinction of head and tail) as the forementioned stone at the entry of the cave.

Lhwyd's 'cave' was in fact a vault of overhanging or corbelled slabs, each placed horizontally on the one below and overlapping slightly so that the space between the chamber walls progressively narrows up to the single closing stone, very nearly 20 feet from the floor below. The visitor who stands underneath this spot today finds himself at the heart of one of the most intriguing mysteries of prehistoric Europe. How were the huge boulders manoeuvred up with such precision that they have remained in perfect balance without mortar for over 4,000 years? What was the purpose of those three elaborately hewn basins, now restored to their proper place in each of the three recesses of the chamber? Why is there such a deliberate twist in the narrow passage which leads the visitor for over 60 feet through the mound? Above all, what is the meaning of the strange spirals, loops and triangles outlined on the stones?

The carvings range from such carefully planned and executed designs as the three entwined spirals by the end recess, to crude circles and

5. Looking up at the corbelled roof of the chamber at Newgrange.

meandering zig-zags scratched at random on the encircling kerb of stones along the edge of the mound. The vision behind these patterns seems quite different from the vivid representational art of the European cave painters. Newgrange reproduces the eerie atmosphere of those primitive caverns but we cannot recognize the forms of hunted animals among the curves and chevrons of the tomb. This art is abstract, and surely it must also be symbolic of values too sacred or intricate to express by images of ordinary reality.

The Modern Evidence

Archaeologists cannot answer all our questions but as a result of the recent work of excavating and restoring the tomb, directed by Professor O'Kelly, much of the background can be filled in. For example, 3 analysis of buried pollen has shown that some forest clearance and wheat

6. A detail from the roofstone over the right-hand recess at Newgrange.

cultivation had taken place in the Boyne valley by the time of the erection of the tomb, but that the area was now reverting to its wooded state. The radiocarbon dating method established this time very roughly as 2500 BC. Possibly the first step was the decoration and building of the passage and chamber as a free-standing structure, enclosed under a special cairn of stones. These stones were carefully selected, round water-rolled boulders, not simply rubble removed from the nearest convenient quarry. In fact the major slabs which form the uprights and roofing stones of the passage and chamber—and there are over 300 of these—are all high quality, weathered glacial boulders, which must have been brought from considerable distances, perhaps several miles, to the site. The assembly of the construction material must have been as formidable a task as the actual erection of the tomb.

After the completion of the essential core of Newgrange, the next likely stage would be the setting out of a series of upright megaliths, some of them over 8 feet tall, in a ring approximately 340 feet in diameter. Inside this ring was a continuous line of 97 large slabs placed on their sides to form an oval perimeter to the mound, flattened near the entrance, with an axis roughly coinciding with the passage centre line. Of the kerbstones so far revealed, many have inconspicuous decoration, some of it scratched in profusion on the backs of the stones, facing the mound where it would never have been seen. Only three bear ornament of any quality, the most impressive being the two great

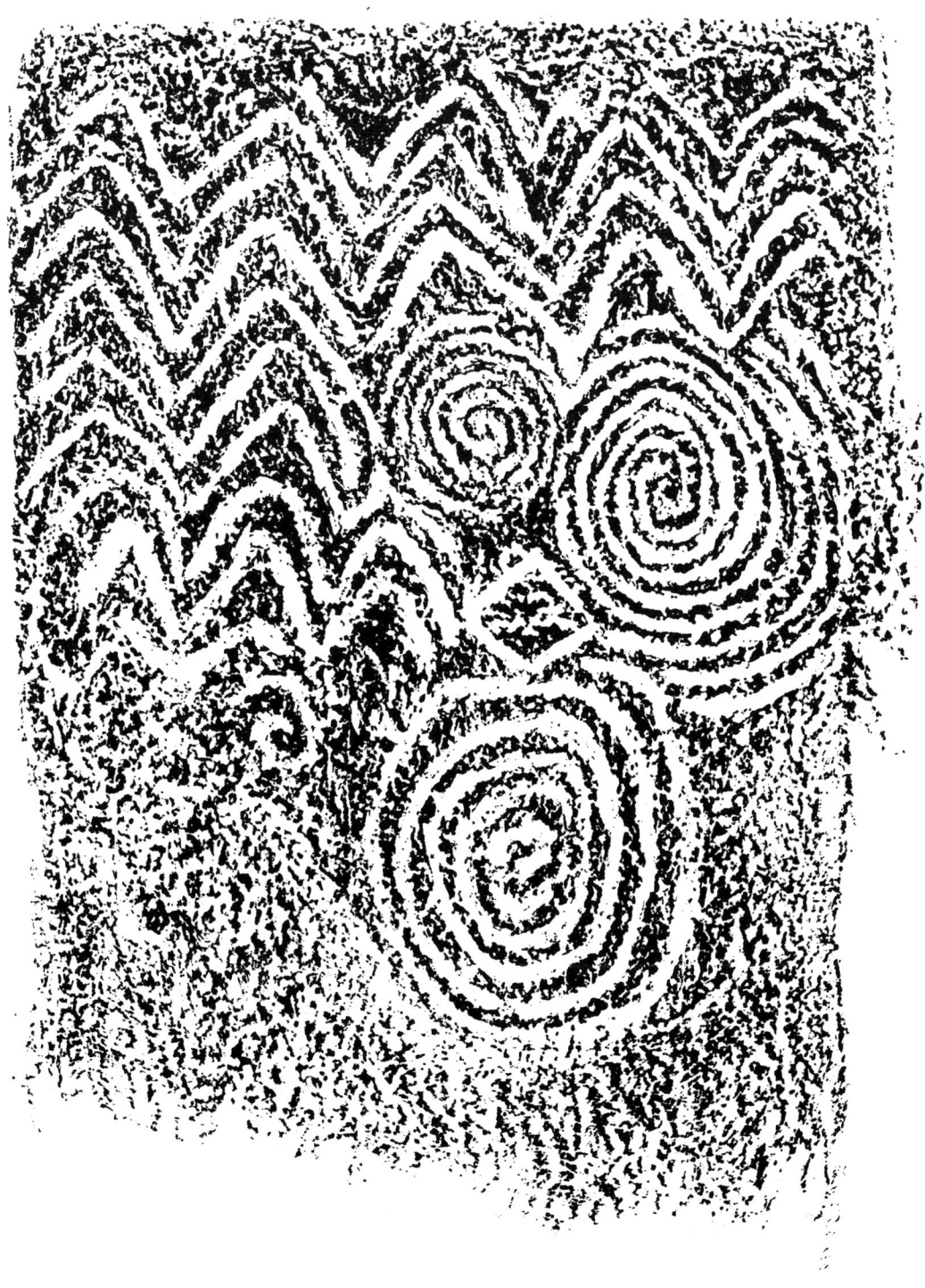

7. A rubbing of the carving on a passage upright (L.19) at Newgrange. Carving area about 22 × 16 ins)56 × 40 cm).

stones which seem to mark the axis of the mound. The famous Entrance Stone with its deeply worked swirling lines, which flow smoothly over its contours and twist into arcs and spirals, is the most perfectly composed stone in the Boyne valley. Artistic confidence of a high order is obvious from the skilled control of the spiral sizes, the lozenges which break up and balance the design, and the outer waves that emphasize the main motifs. With this stone, Newgrange gives us an insight not merely into the scope of ancient labour resources but also into the vigour of the prehistoric imagination.

When complete, the tomb would have appeared as a flat-topped cone some 40 feet high, crowning the ridge of the Boyne with its nearly vertical front facade of granite boulders and gleaming white quartz. It is hardly surprising that this monument, even in a dilapidated state, became a legendary subject for the storytellers of pre-Christian times.

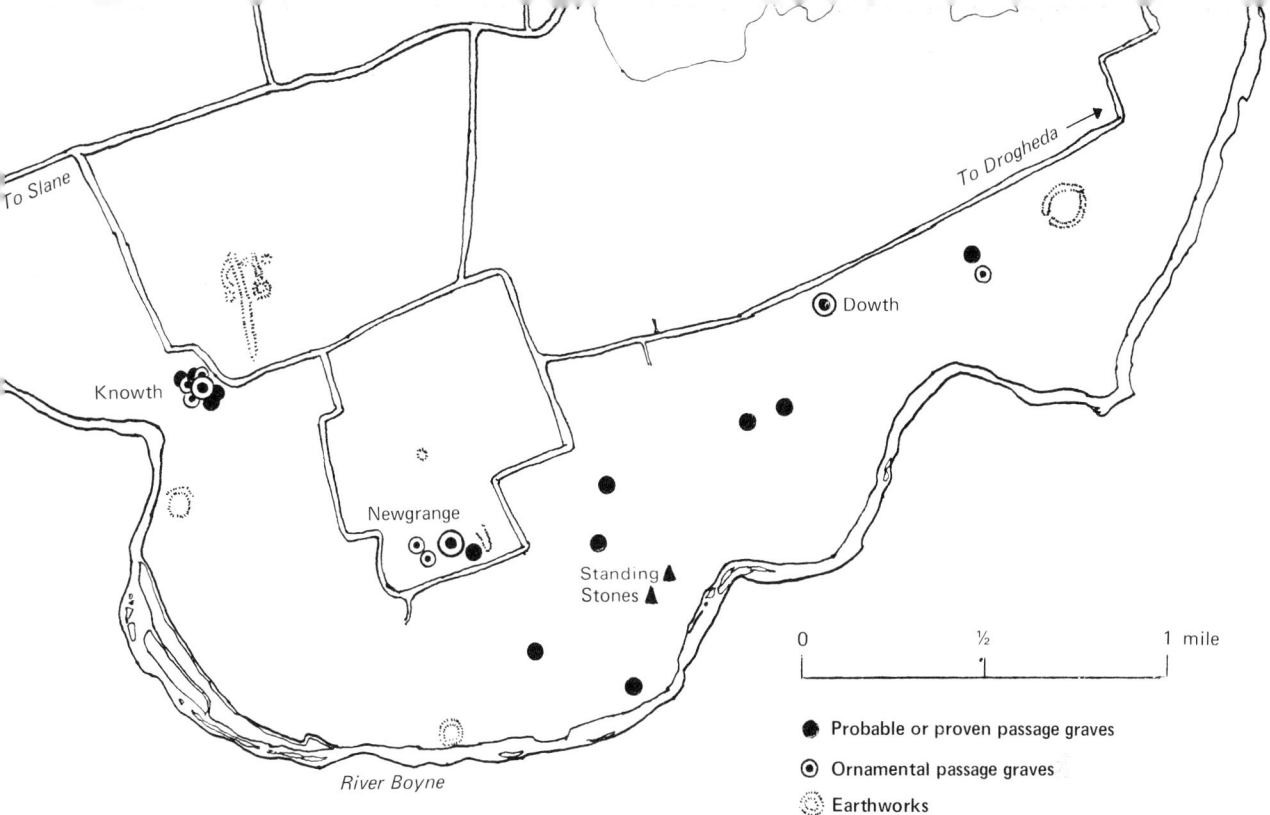

Knowth

To Slane

To Drogheda

Dowth

Newgrange

Standing ▲
Stones ▲

River Boyne

0   ½   1 mile

● Probable or proven passage graves

◉ Ornamental passage graves

Earthworks

9. Plan of the major sites
at the bend of the Boyne,
Co. Meath.

Within a mile and a half radius of Newgrange stand two mounds of comparable size, still known by their ancient names of Knowth and Dowth. The opening of Dowth took place in 1847 with the help of machinery used for boring wells, and the results were inadequately recorded. But two passage graves were discovered in the south-west sector of the mound, one of cruciform plan with the remains of a stone basin and several subsidiary chambers connected to the right-hand recess. The carvings discovered at Dowth are in complete contrast to the major designs of Newgrange. The motifs are lightly picked into the stone and are scattered more or less at random, similar to the hidden ornament of the Newgrange kerbstones. The most interesting carving, fully revealed during conservation work twenty years ago, is the face of a kerbstone on the eastern side of Dowth. The average visitor would have no trouble in identifying seven 'suns' on this stone, and indeed this is perhaps the only case in the whole range of the Boyne art where a representational meaning seems at all convincing.

For over a decade the mound of Knowth has been extensively investigated by a team of archaeologists led by Dr George Eogan. The task was a formidable one: to reveal the history of a mound nearly 300 feet

4

5

11

10. Detail of 'sun' carvings on a kerbstone at Dowth.

11. How a passage grave may have looked a short time after its completion. This is one of the satellite tombs (Site 4) surrounding the main mound at Knowth, currently under excavation and restoration.

12. One of over a hundred kerbstones lining the base of the main mound at Knowth (Stone 22).

long at its greatest extent, with 15 smaller (or 'satellite') graves clustered around its base. At least two of these minor tombs preceded the construction of the great mound. Excavation showed how the mound had been elaborately built up with alternate bands of stone, clay, shale and turf. This technique probably ensured greater stability than the vertical boulder front of Newgrange, which may have begun to collapse within a short time after completion. The vast 'layer cake' of Knowth was eventually piled up to a height of at least 36 feet. Around its perimeter was a line of kerbstones, of which 104 have been identified out of a probable total of 140. The great majority of these bear decoration in a self-assured and balanced style, covering the whole surface of the slab and reminiscent of the Entrance Stone at Newgrange, but not of the rest of the Newgrange decoration. The profusion of gapped circles, meandering 'serpent' lines and 'U' patterns differs from the prominence of the lozenge and spiral at Newgrange.

Where was the passage of the Knowth tomb to be found? The early antiquaries had failed to make any headway through the huge mass of

13

13/14. The magnificent carved stone bowl, found broken in the right-hand recess of the Knowth tomb discovered in 1968.

earth and rubble. Preliminary investigation by Professor Macalister in 1943 also failed to disclose an entrance, and it was only in July 1967 that a passage was discovered on the western side, at a point (just as at Newgrange) where the line of kerbstones swung inwards for a short distance. In front of the entrance was a decorated stone with a vertical line reminiscent of Newgrange, and a remarkable pattern of rectangles boxed in by one another. Behind this, the passage stretched into the mound for an immense length—about 113 feet, nearly double the Newgrange distance—with a twist to the right about three-quarters of the way along. It led to a rectangular chamber only about four feet wide and seven feet high, with a back wall stone which reproduced the pattern of the entrance stone, with the exception of the vertical line. In all some 28 decorated stones were discovered inside the tomb.

With such a successful discovery behind them, it came as a considerable surprise to the excavators when another passage grave was found in the autumn of 1968, this time with an entrance at the east diametrically opposite to the first and again indicated by an inward bulge in the kerb. The present evidence suggests that both tombs were built at the same time. The straight passage led to a cruciform chamber so placed that the rear slabs of the 1967 and 1968 tombs stood very nearly back-to-back, separated only by some ten feet of mound material. In this chamber, the archaeologists found a carved basin lying partly broken in the right-hand recess, with a bold pattern of rays and semi-circles on its upper surface. A series of horizontal grooves run right around the outside of the bowl, interrupted by a design of concentric circles on one face. This is perhaps the most striking object ever found inside a prehistoric chambered tomb.

The People of the Tombs

Even at Knowth, the contents of the tombs had been disturbed by early intruders, probably long before the Vikings who were recorded as plundering the 'caves' of Knowth and Dowth in 861/2 AD. The excavation of the Newgrange chamber in 1967 produced the fragmentary remains of some four or five individuals embedded in the floor, and this was surely a small fraction of the original burial deposits in this much-disturbed tomb. Much of our knowledge of the material possessions of the passage grave builders in fact comes from outside the Boyne valley, notably from the clearing out of the Loughcrew cairns which took place in the last century.

The Loughcrew cemetery did not attract the attentions of antiquarians until the 9th of June 1863, when a local schoolmaster named Eugene Alfred Conwell took his wife for a picnic on the hill known as Sliabh na Caillighe, the Hill of the Witch, 25 miles west of the Boyne. Conwell described how

'to my great astonishment, I found this commanding site studded with the remains of a necropolis of pre-historic age . . . When I first stated that I had discovered a series of hitherto unnoticed and undescribed cairns, established for 2 miles along a range of hills, within 40 miles of the city of Dublin, I was laughed at, naturally enough . . .'.

Undeterred, Conwell named each of the 29 cairns he had discovered with an alphabetical letter and set about the operation of removing the rubble with the help of a gang of workmen. Their task met certain obstacles, chief of which was the largest mound of the entire series, cairn D, which required about 28 paces for the visitor to reach the top. After two weeks' work by a dozen labourers who drove a huge trench through the rubble from east to west, the land surface had still not been reached nor had any trace of a passage been found. Conwell abandoned the attempt and decided that D was a cenotaph not intended for the purposes of burial.

At the other sites, he was much more successful. One of the most important tombs of the cemetery, cairn L, yielded up a stone basin nearly six feet broad, under which were found 900 charred pieces of bone, 48 teeth and a number of polished stone balls all less than three inches in diameter. Conwell described eight of them as white, one as made of syenite, one of brown and another of purple and white stone. These 'marbles' were found at many other passage grave sites, including Newgrange. Perhaps they should be considered along with the obvious taste for trinkets and decorative dress fasteners apparent from the burials. Beads and perforated stone pendants, often in the shape of small hammers, are common, and so, too, are fragmentary bone pins which were sometimes over a foot long when originally made. It is possible that these pins were intended for fastening clothes or hair, but it has also been suggested that they were used to close up leather or cloth bags full of cremated bone and funerary objects deposited in the tomb.

The accumulated evidence of excavations shows that collective burial of men, women and children, mostly cremated, was the accepted

. The west recess and its corated lintel at the Four-ocks passage grave, Co. eath.

practice, and that the tombs continued to be used for successive rites. The purpose of the basins was probably to contain cremated remains, although several cases are known of evenly distributed layers of bone up to six inches thick spread all over the chamber. At the Fourknocks tomb, some 15 miles south-east of Newgrange, the remains of over 100 individuals were found deposited in the passageway and in the three recesses. It seems natural to regard the passage graves as the communal burial vaults of important families who commanded the respect or obedience of those who helped to build the tomb.

16/17. Detail of two carved uprights in the passage of Cairn T, Loughcrew.

18/19. A stone from Cairn L, Loughcrew, which dominates the main recess, and a slab from a recess in Cairn T. Both carvings have been chalked in by previous visitors.

This speculation may lead us to ask more difficult questions about the beliefs which the material remains seem to attest. The simplest assumption is that the presence of everyday objects like buttons, beads and pins indicates a belief in a reproduction of the living world after death. To some the cave or womb-like atmosphere of many tombs suggests a place of rebirth. Recent evidence from Newgrange indicates that these ideas may not wholly be the product of modern imagination.

During the excavation of the mound, Professor O'Kelly was faced 8 with the problem of explaining a small gap in the structure of the roof not far from the entrance, seemingly emphasized by a box-like arrangement of slabs angled above it. This constructional feature was evidently not intended to be blocked over by mound material because the front edge of the uppermost slab was finely decorated with a lozenge and rectangle pattern. Why should the builders have left a deliberate slot open above the entrance when it is clear that the tomb mouth itself was sealed by a blocking slab? Was the so-called 'roof-box' intended to allow spirits to escape, or was it intended to let something *in*?

The Professor discovered by on-the-spot observations that, a few minutes after dawn at the winter solstice, the shortest day of the year, the sun rises directly in line with the entrance of Newgrange. Furthermore, the light penetrates not merely through the slot of the roof-box and the passage roof, but down the full length of the twisting passageway to the rear edge of the basin stone in the end recess, nearly 70 feet away. So, every winter at this traditional time of pagan festival and renewal, a thin beam of light crept into the darkness of Newgrange and briefly touched the basin where cremated bodies must have lain, overlooked by the triple spiral carving.

The Hidden Symbols

We have already seen that each of the main Boyne tombs—Newgrange, Knowth and Dowth—has its own distinctive style of carving. Perhaps the simplest way of explaining the differences is to imagine that the passage graves were not all contemporary but succeeded one another over quite a long period. The inferior quality of the stone used at Knowth, Dowth and elsewhere suggests that all the best glacial material was used up in the construction of Newgrange. Another radiocarbon date obtained for a passage grave (The Mound of the Hostages at Tara) of about 2100 BC shows that passage graves were still being built several 9 centuries after Newgrange was completed. So the different art styles

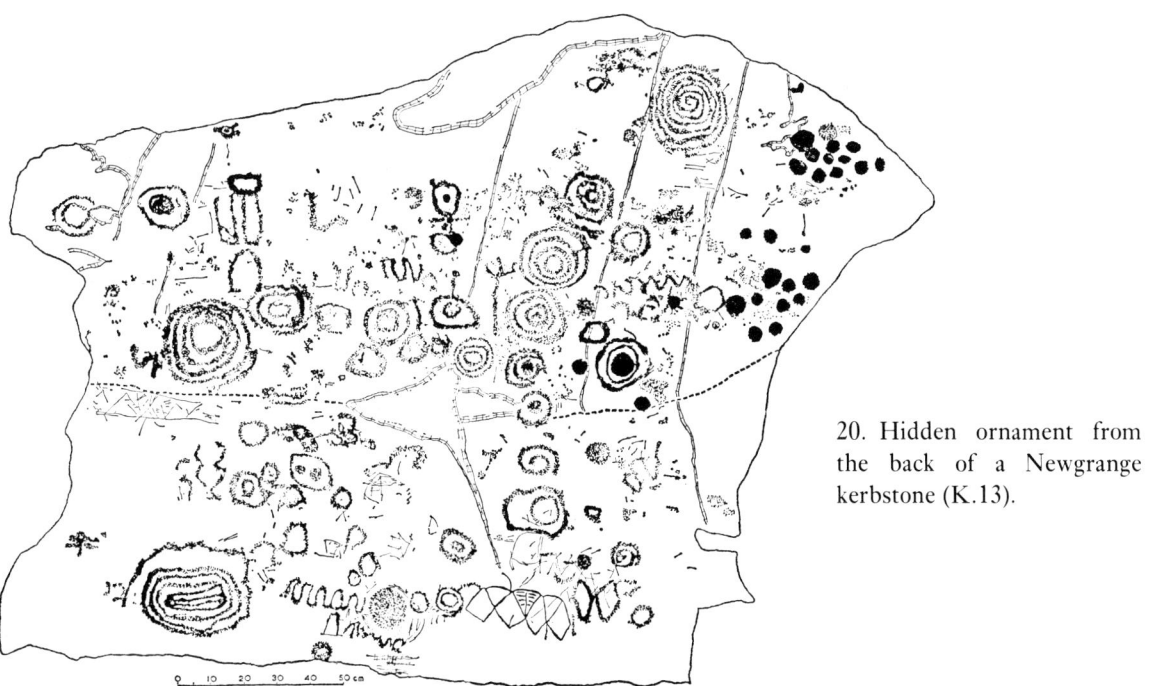

20. Hidden ornament from the back of a Newgrange kerbstone (K.13).

and techniques of the Boyne valley could have evolved over a long period of time.

This explanation does not account, however, for contrasts within the structure of a single tomb. Why did the builders of Newgrange decorate the *backs* of the kerbstones and the *upper* faces of roof slabs in a completely different style to the major ornament of the tomb? The systematic arrangement and excellent workmanship of the visible designs is absent from these hidden surfaces, some of which are covered with a chaos of dots, circles, zig-zags and spirals lightly pocked or scratched into the stone. The decoration of a few kerb-backs is so random that it almost looks like graffiti perhaps carved at idle moments by labourers during the construction of the tomb. Could these stones have been removed from another earlier monument, or have been practice 'sketchbooks' for the artists who set to work on the 'official' designs?

The excavations showed that in certain cases both the formal and informal carvings were executed as the monument was under construction. Moreover the 'graffiti' do not seem to be either preliminary sketches for, or crude copies of, the visible ornament. The circle and dot are the commonest designs, while the lozenge and zig-zag are only occasionally present. So the different styles also involve a different set

21

21. Looking from the end recess at Newgrange towards the chamber and passage. The view of the camera almost coincides with the astronomical alignment through the roof-box.

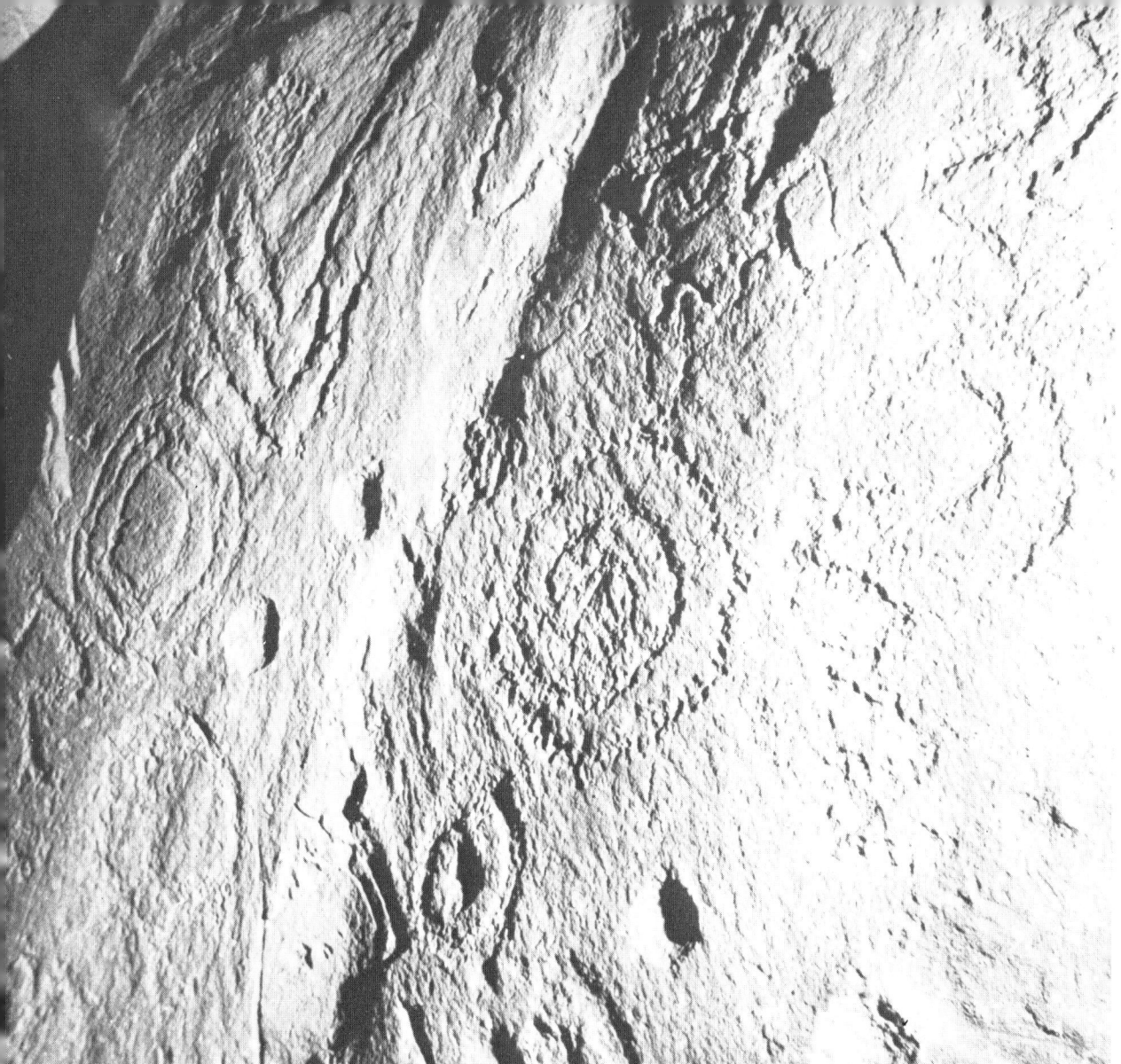

of symbols.

The impact of the most elaborate Newgrange stones, such as the Entrance Stone, the rear kerb and the triple spiral, is so great that the visitor would expect the spiral to come top of the list of repeated motifs at the tomb. Yet if the contrasting hidden ornament is considered as well as the main designs, the spiral comes fourth in order of frequency, preceded by the lozenge, zig-zag and circle, and followed by the 'serpent', dot and concentric circles. So pinning down a specific Newgrange style may be a more difficult task than a casual visitor might suppose.

22. Detail of the hidden ornament on the back of a chamber stone in a satellite tomb at Knowth (Site 2). These carvings were completely covered by the material of the mound.

10

24

Indeed the contrast between formal and informal decoration is not confined to one tomb. Although the frequency of motifs presents a complicated picture and deserves careful study, the whole of passage grave art seems to reflect these differences. Miss Elizabeth Shee has 11 defined quite a narrow range of 16 basic motifs which apply to all the decorated Irish tombs. But the elaborately conceived panels of ornament at Newgrange, Knowth and Fourknocks seem to exclude patterns which are very common elsewhere. For example, wherever we find patterns carved haphazardly on the stone—like Dowth, the Knowth satellite tombs, the hidden stones of Newgrange, and most of the passage graves outside the Boyne valley—the circle is the commonest symbol. Similarly the 'sun' or 'flower', and parallel lines, are fairly common at Loughcrew and elsewhere but not at Newgrange, Knowth or Fourknocks. Why are the motifs missing from the carefully planned designs of these Boyne tombs?

A simple chronological distinction, perhaps a time gap of decades or centuries, might explain it all, since doubtless old motifs were forgotten and new ones invented. But this cannot quite account for the details of the picture. At Newgrange the lozenge occurs on over 40 per cent of all the carved stones, while at Loughcrew and other sites, it is present on only just over 10 per cent. Yet Newgrange, Knowth and Dowth share one motif (variously called the 'offset', 'fir tree' or 'ship' design) with Loughcrew, where it appears on 15 stones, and with no other site outside the Boyne valley. It is difficult to make sense of these distinctions. Perhaps they are merely the result of the preferences of individual passage grave artists. Yet careful analysis of the carvings clearly raises as many questions as it solves.

How Were They Carved?

No metal object has ever been found as part of the original burial deposit 12 in a passage grave, and indeed the date of Newgrange places it some centuries before the use of copper and bronze tools became common. All the tomb carvings could have been produced by repeated blows from a variety of pointed or square-edged flint tools. Sometimes, as at Dowth and Fourknocks, simple scratched or incised lines were made to sketch out the pattern before the major carving began. The design might be outlined by continuous picked grooves or by removing a solid area of background so that the effect of 'false relief' was obtained. Somewhat cruder treatment was used to shape and smooth the surfaces of the

Newgrange passage and chamber. Most of this shaping seems to have taken place after the construction of the tomb and, curiously, in some cases seems intended to obliterate ornament previously applied. Why a few carvings were erased and the others preserved is another of the puzzles of Newgrange.

The Spread of Passage Grave Art

The values expressed by megalithic art were not confined to eastern Ireland. Even as far north as the Orkney island of Eday, a twin pair of spirals from a ruined cairn seems to witness the influence of passage grave traditions. It is clear that the Irish Sea played an important part in prehistoric times not merely in the circulation of trade but in the spread of artistic and religious ideas. We should not be surprised, therefore, to find that two major cruciform passage graves were built in Anglesey, one of them at the site known as Bryn Celli Ddu. Here the 13 builders chose to construct their tomb over an earlier stone circle. At the centre of the previous monument they left two stone slabs, one decorated with a continuous meandering line winding over the upper, lower and one of the side surfaces. This slab might have been placed

24. A stone from the island of Eday, Orkney.

as an act of propitiation or dedication. A small spiral was also carved inside the tomb on a chamber upright.

The other Anglesey passage grave at Barclodiad y Gawres overlooks   14
the Irish Sea. Five decorated stones were discovered during the excavation in 1952/3, carved with spirals, lozenges, zig-zags and chevrons in a style very close to that of Newgrange. The most striking of these ornamented panels has frequently been compared to a human figure. It features a band of zig-zags placed below a much-weathered spiral and framing a central lozenge. The triangular and U-shaped 'arms' along the sides of the stone may remind us of another supposedly human carving at Fourknocks. Whether these designs are regarded as idols depends on wider subjective ideas about the meaning of passage grave art. As Professor O'Kelly has warned,

'It is too easy for a modern sophisticated imagination to see faces or figures where neither were intended by those who carved the patterns.'

Besides the slab from Eday, no imposingly decorated stone occurs in the passage graves of northern and western Scotland, despite the influence which the architecture and tradition of the Boyne must have exerted. In the finest of all the northern tombs, Maes Howe, which is situated on the Orkney mainland and surely owes its cruciform plan to Irish traditions, the only marks on the huge walling slabs were left by Norsemen who broke in during the 1150's, described their adventures in dozens of runic inscriptions and made small incised drawings. Indeed the only carvings which seem to reflect Boyne influences outside Ireland and Anglesey are not found along the Atlantic coastlines at all, but are distributed mainly in the central Scottish lowlands and along the east coasts of Scotland and England. 16 These are the decorated covers of simple box-like graves or cists (intended for single burial) which are traditionally assigned to the Bronze Age—perhaps as much as a millennium after the construction of Newgrange. On the cover of a grave from Carnwath, Lanarkshire, for example, is a group of concentric circles set beside triangle motifs. A large proportion of these decorated covers are awkwardly shaped for the cists which they were intended to close, while their circular designs are often interrupted by the edges of the stone. This probably indicates that they are broken-up slabs re-used by the single grave builders at a later period. It seems that the symbols remotely connected with the great Irish tombs continued to be respected over a wide area for many generations.

The same conclusion emerges from consideration of a variety of small objects decorated in 'the passage grave style'. Spiral motifs have been found on pottery at the great ceremonial site of Durrington Walls, 17 less than two miles away from Stonehenge. A spirally decorated object, carved from antler and perforated as if for mounting on a haft or handle, was recovered from beneath a river bank near Garboldisham in Norfolk. 18 Then from east Yorkshire come three striking objects, again without any obvious functional use, carved out of chalk into drum-like shapes about 4–5 inches across. The elaborately carved 'Folkton Drums', 19 covered with triangles, lozenges and concentric circles, were found together in the grave of a five-year old child. But perhaps the most extraordinary of all these isolated discoveries are the carved stone balls

28

25. The Fourknocks 'face' carving.

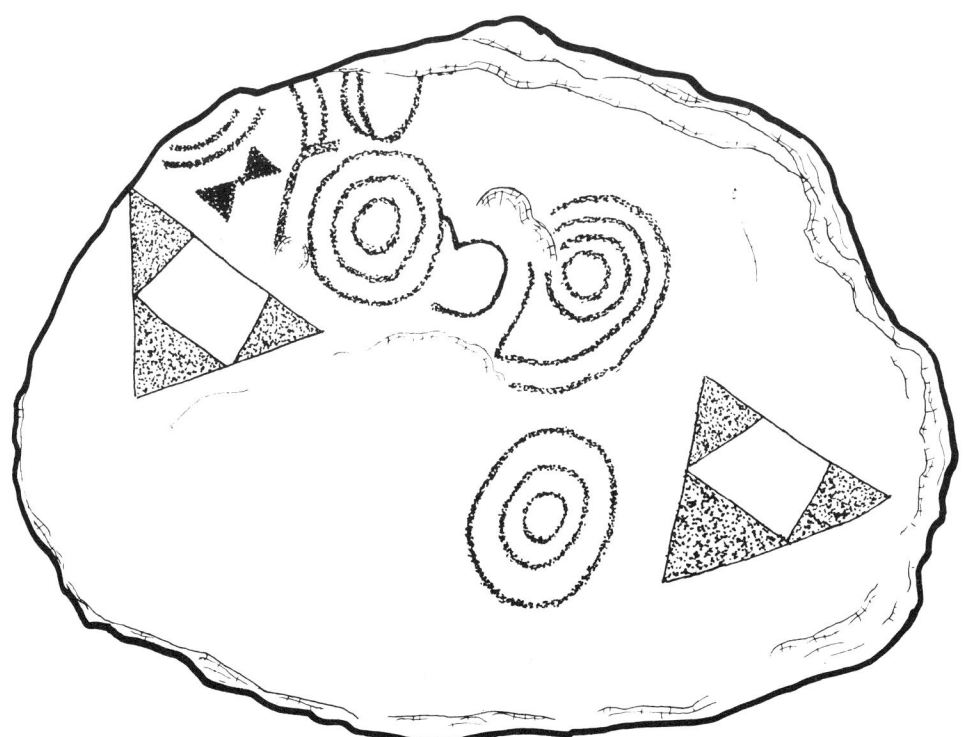

6. A sketch of the cover from single grave at Carnwath, Lanarkshire, decorated in 'the passage grave style'. One-foot scale shown.

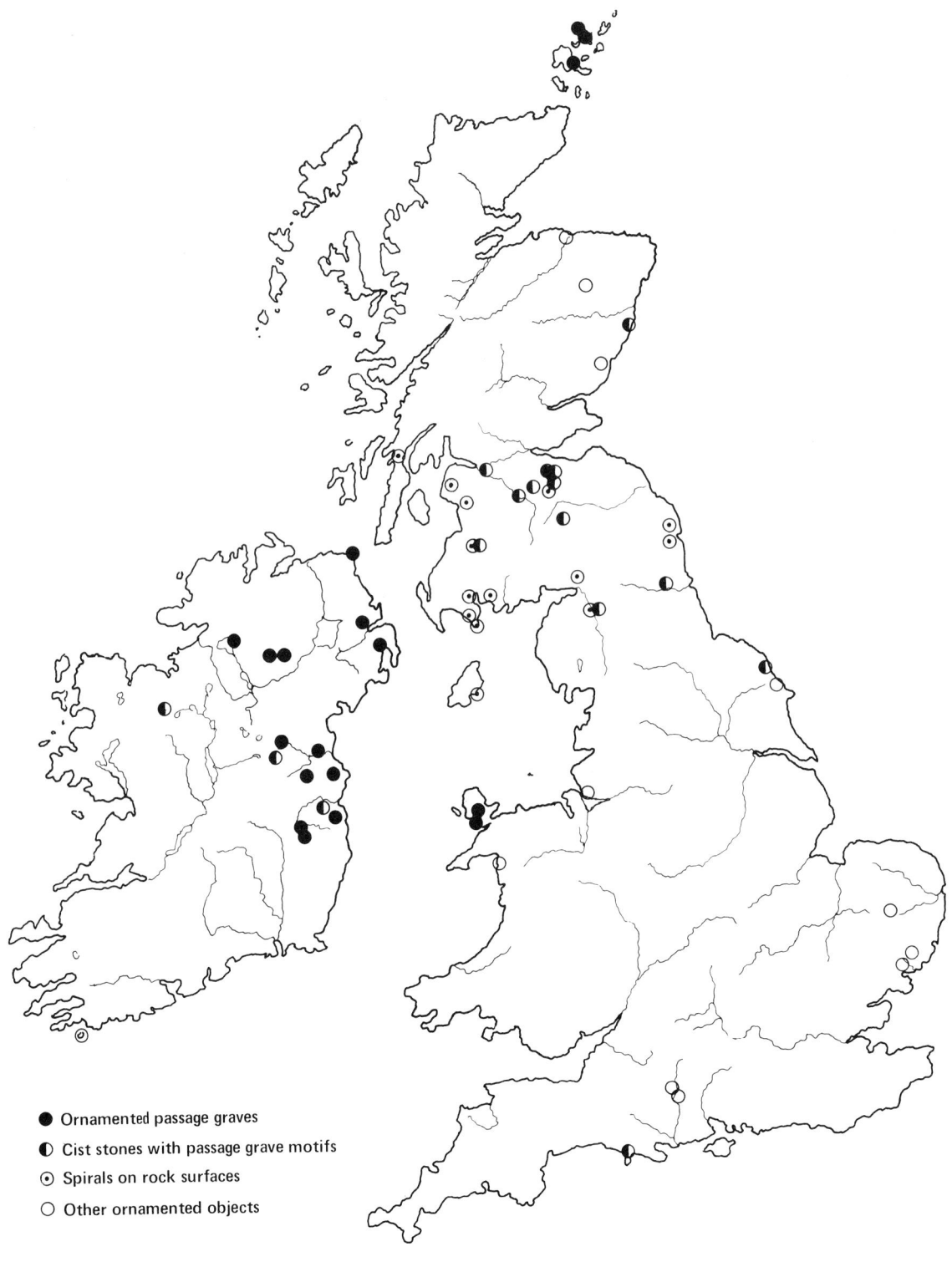

27. Map of passage grave art and its influence.

● Ornamented passage graves

◐ Cist stones with passage grave motifs

⊙ Spirals on rock surfaces

○ Other ornamented objects

28/29. One of the three carved chalk drums from Folkton, Yorkshire. Several different sources have been claimed for the style of decoration on these strange objects.

of eastern Scotland, notably the example uncovered in 1860 at Towie, Aberdeenshire. This is about three inches in diameter and has four projecting knob-like faces densely patterned with double spirals, chevrons, serpentine lines and concentric circles. It is difficult to believe that this combination of patterns so similar to the repertoire of the Boyne was coincidentally applied to this strange object.

The evidence from the single graves and the chance finds seems to show that the symbols which decorated the stones of the great Irish tombs had a significance that was appreciated throughout a wide area of ancient Britain. We can only guess how the motifs found their way over such long distances. One plausible suggestion is that the designs were in fact worn as tattooed or painted body ornament. 20

These thoughts on the far-ranging meaning of the passage grave art lead us to a crucial question: was this style introduced from sources outside Britain, or did it develop independently?

Origin of the Tombs

Newgrange, Loughcrew and the other Irish tombs are part of a burial tradition which was widespread along the Atlantic coastline of Europe.

From the Orkneys south to the shores of Brittany, Portugal and south-eastern Spain, are located groups sharing the features of a chamber and passage built from large stones or megaliths, covered over with a circular mound of earth. Some impress the visitor no less than the Boyne sites: monuments such as Maes Howe, built of sandstone slabs up to 25 feet long, or the profusely carved Gavrinis in southern Brittany, its stones entirely covered by rippling lines and arcs. For over a century the widely scattered tombs have been the focus of intensive study and argument by prominent figures in European archaeology—men such as Montelius, Leeds, Obermaier, Gordon Childe, Daniel and Renfrew, who all had their own particular view of how the megalithic tradition began, often conflicting with the previous authorities.   21

Up to a few years ago, these studies were almost entirely concerned with establishing sequences of development both within and between the groups of monuments by the small variations in their plans and structure, together with comparisons of the different grave goods. The most elaborate constructions could then be seen as evolving from the simpler forms, or, alternatively, it could be argued that the crudest tombs were later, degenerate copies of the finest monuments. To a layman these discussions concerned with intricate classifications of pottery and tomb styles often seem pedantic and self-defeating. Yet the experts were trying to answer some fundamental questions: Who built the first monuments in Europe? Where did the movement begin?

The Iberian peninsula was a favourite battleground for these disputes.   22
Were the complex corbelled tombs of Southern Iberia to be derived from the simple chambers without passages common in northern Portugal, as Obermaier and Bosch-Gimpera argued? Others, such as Fleure and Gordon Childe, questioned the assumption that simple architecture and an absence of metal objects in the northern tombs necessarily meant that they were earlier. So completely contradictory theories could be held about the origin of the Iberian tombs.

But another possibility also presented itself, that the chamber and passage tomb was not a native development at all but was introduced from the outside. In particular, there seemed to be a possible connection between the drystone tombs of southern Crete and monuments of the Spanish group. A more tangible link with the Aegean was the female cult figure which was carved or painted on the walls of the Iberian tombs, and which appeared on small stone or bone objects and on certain types of pottery. Surely this was the same deity whose image found its most

33

perfect expression in the famous Cycladic carved figures—the 'Mother Goddess' herself?

The concept of missionaries arriving with new gods in an alien land has a stronger appeal to the imagination than the dry typologies of megalithic structures. It is not hard to account for the acceptance of views like those vigorously argued by Elliot Smith that the Egyptian 'Children of the Sun' (as his disciple Perry titled a book of 1923) had populated the whole of Europe and introduced every technological and artistic advance. The concept that the world was once colonized by one master civilization, or by an invasion of spacemen, is still popular today.

More down-to-earth theorists were nevertheless able to make a convincing case for the spread or 'diffusion' of the passage grave religion from the Near East to the Atlantic seaways, from Spain to Brittany and so on to the Boyne and Orkney. The spirals of Newgrange were surely distant and barbaric copies of the spirals found carved on the grave slabs of Homer's Mycenae. What was the high corbelled vault of Newgrange itself but a rough-hewn imitation of the soaring beehive tombs could be found than these magnificently engineered structures? after 1500 BC? What better prototypes for the chamber and passage tombs, built of fine masonry close by the citadel of Mycenae, sometime

31. A typical decorated plaque from an Iberian passage grave.

A further convincing point in favour of this argument was that the actual colonies of the missionary traders could be identified in southern Spain. At a site such as Los Millares in south-east Spain, a fortified citadel had been established at least by 2500 BC, complete with a cemetery of 75 tombs just outside its walls. Differences in the material goods found in townships such as Los Millares and Vila Nova compared to sites in their surrounding inland area encouraged the view that these were the colonies of the new settlers, fortified against a hostile indigenous population. Eventually the new creed was absorbed by the natives, and tombs began to be built over a wide area of the peninsula.

Yet such a neat solution to the problem of the megaliths was vulnerable to criticism. Could the special quality of the remains found inside the townships simply reflect the concentration of wealth within these developing urban communities? Renfrew was able to show the question-

23

able basis of many of the parallels with the Aegean, and to suggest that allegedly 'colonialist' pottery, copper metal-working and chambered tombs might all be the products of local invention and development. Indeed, while such exotic objects as ostrich egg beads and ivory combs and sandles clearly indicated imports from north Africa, there was a complete absence of similar luxury goods from the eastern Mediterranean.

An even more serious objection to the entire framework of megalithic origins began to emerge with the first radiocarbon dates processed from the finds of the chamber tombs. The radiocarbon method permits rough dating, usually to within a century or two on either side of the quoted figure. Even allowing for the possible inaccuracies of the system, the dates for Breton tombs such as Barnenez (3800 BC ± 150) or Kercado (3880 BC ± 300) are very much older than the conventional framework allowed if they had been ultimately inspired by the tombs of the Aegean. Newgrange itself, now dated to about 2500 BC, is at least a thousand years or more older than the grave slabs of Mycenae, which were supposed to have inspired its art. From the handful of dates so far available it would be unwise to reach any firm conclusions, but at the moment it seems that the earliest chamber and passage tombs in Europe are to be found in Brittany, and not in Iberia or the Aegean. 24

Natives or Colonists?

The lessons of the colonialist theory suggest some questions which are relevant to the Irish tombs and their carvings. Can we agree with the conventional view that envisages an influx of traders and settlers arriving in the Boyne area from Brittany or Spain sometime before 2500 BC? In other words, is the evidence of the Irish tomb building culture sufficiently distinctive to indicate a colony established from outside, or can we imagine the people of the Boyne independently inventing their own special traditions of art and burial?

The basic structure of the Irish monuments—the passage, chamber and round mound—indicates that they have some connection, however distant, with the ideas of tomb builders in Iberia and Brittany. Excavations at Knowth and other Irish sites seems to show that 'undifferentiated' passage graves (where the chamber is hardly more than a continuation of the passage) were built at the same period as the classic cruciform types. Similarly in Brittany and Spain, the undifferentiated style appears to be contemporary with more conventional structures, and this reinforces the impression of close connections. However, despite similarities with some Iberian tombs, the typical cruciform plan of Newgrange or Loughcrew has no precise parallel anywhere further south in Europe, and so to some extent seems to represent a distinct achievement in terms of megalithic architecture. 25

The same sort of qualified picture emerges from a consideration of the art. The bands of zig-zag decoration prominent at Newgrange and Fourknocks are very close to the patterns on the little 'goddess'

32. View of the entrance to the so-called Treasury of Atreus, leading to a remarkable beehive-shaped chamber. This is one of a number of tombs built close to the citadel of Mycenae, Greece, sometime after 1500 BC.

figures of southern Portugal, the stone or bone plaques with their multiple chevron designs. If this is a real connection, however, we might expect a wider distribution of the plaques outside Iberia, perhaps even finds in Ireland itself. In fact it is only on a few Boyne stones that these panels of zig-zag ornament are combined with other motifs to suggest anything remotely like a full human figure. Spiral carvings are almost completely absent from the Iberian tombs, and indeed the closest comparisons come from patterns on a few isolated rock surfaces.

It is equally surprising to find that there are only four spiral carvings in Brittany, all inconspicuous examples from among the mass of decoration on the stones of Gavrinis. Widespread motifs in Brittany, such as axe carvings and a type of 'goddess' figure more recognizable as such than any of the Irish designs, are almost entirely missing from the Boyne tombs. Moreover, Gavrinis and Petit Mont, which provide the closest approach to the artistic feeling behind much of the Newgrange decoration, are often considered as exceptional and perhaps late among the Brittany series. So those four spirals are quite possibly the result of influence from the Boyne rather than the other way round.

In the case of Knowth, there is again no exact outside parallel for the dominant motif of the kerbstones, the continuous or gapped concentric

33. A decorated lintel from the Fourknocks passage grave, Co. Meath.

26

27

34. A view of one of the profusely carved uprights in the passage grave of Gavrinis, southern Brittany.

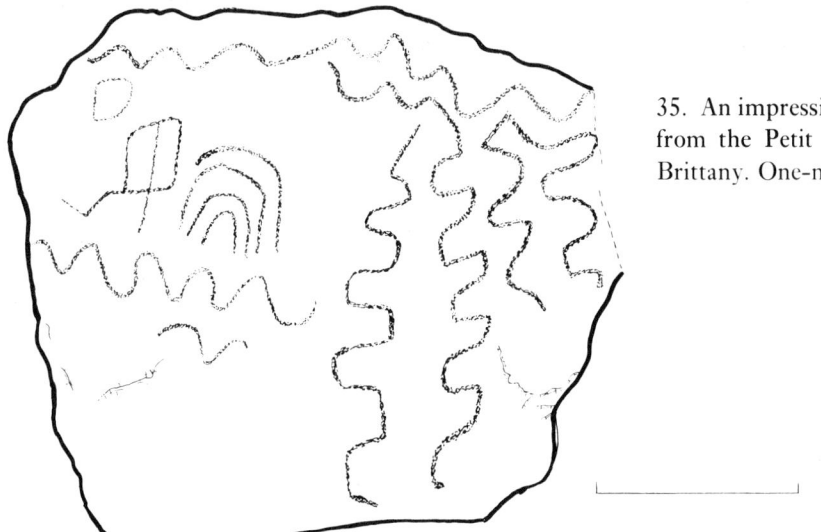

35. An impression of a decorated stone from the Petit Mont tomb, southern Brittany. One-metre scale shown.

circles. But in other respects Knowth does direct our attentions back to Brittany again. The tendency of the kerbstones to be completely covered by a balanced composition is reminiscent of the all-over decoration of Gavrinis. When the first of the Knowth passages was explored in 1967, great surprise was caused by the discovery of a design superimposed over old ornament on the left-hand side of the chamber. 28 Here was a carving precisely similar to the strange 'hafted axe' symbol of the Breton tombs and notably Mané Rutual, repeating such details as the supposed loop attached to the haft and the splayed shape of the blade. At the bend in the passage there was also a design of 'concentric' rectangles, crowned by two circular 'eyes', which is reminiscent of the Breton and Iberian 'goddess' figure. So at Knowth the general impression of limited influences from outside, especially from the megalith builders of Brittany, has been confirmed in the heart of the great mound.

In the face of all the accumulated evidence, any crude idea of a single mass migration to the east of Ireland is unconvincing. The art of each of the major tombs and cemeteries, and indeed of the whole Boyne culture, surely represents a distinctive achievement not likely to have been forced upon a population by an alien power. Instead we may be able to imagine communities in both the Boyne and Brittany which were at least receptive to each other's ideas, perhaps through trading or some kind of closer relationship. Such speculation is less exciting than the purely colonialist theory, and may in the end prove to be just as unfounded. But then we are only at the beginning of serious study of these magnificent burial monuments and their carved rings and spirals, which have fascinated and baffled the visitor for over two and a half centuries.

38

36. The strange carving on the left-hand side of the chamber in the Knowth tomb discovered in 1967. Note the obliteration of previous ornament.

2 Cups and Rings

Carvings on the Crags

The moor slopes of northern England are often dominated by massive rock outcrops which command extensive views of the surrounding landscape. The desolate situation of these crags, where frequently there is no visible sign of human activity in any direction, heightens the surprise of a hiker when he discovers strange patterns carved over the expansive shelves of rock. In such a setting the curious hollows (usually too smooth to be mistaken for natural erosion holes) and their encircling rings are hardly less impressive than the carvings in the

 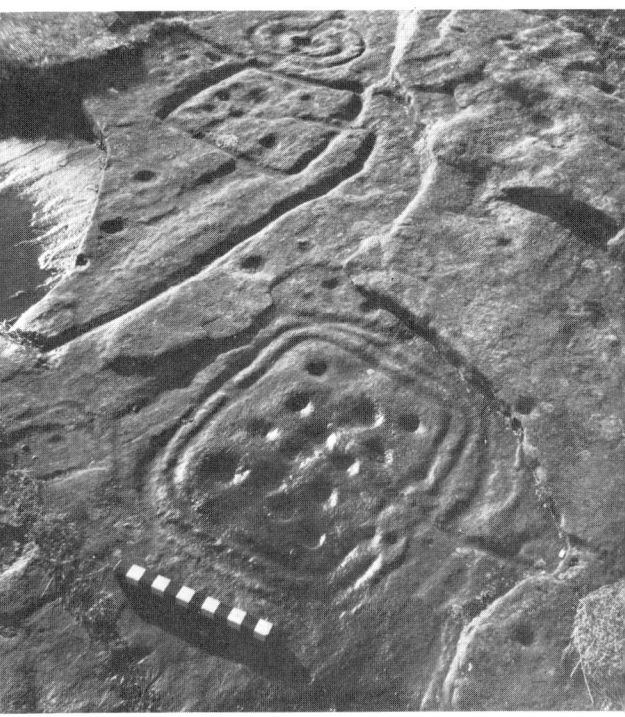

37. The large stone at Dod Law, Northumberland. 38. Another view of the large stone at Dod Law.

man-made tombs. Their weathered condition, however, makes them much more inconspicuous, and probably for this reason they escaped attention until the middle of the last century.

The existence of the cups and rings of Northumberland and Cork–Kerry was reported at about the same time in 1851–52. By chance, also, the first major rocks to be discovered in both regions were situated close by the ruins of impressive forts of the Iron Age period. When the earliest investigators, the Reverend Charles Graves in Ireland and the

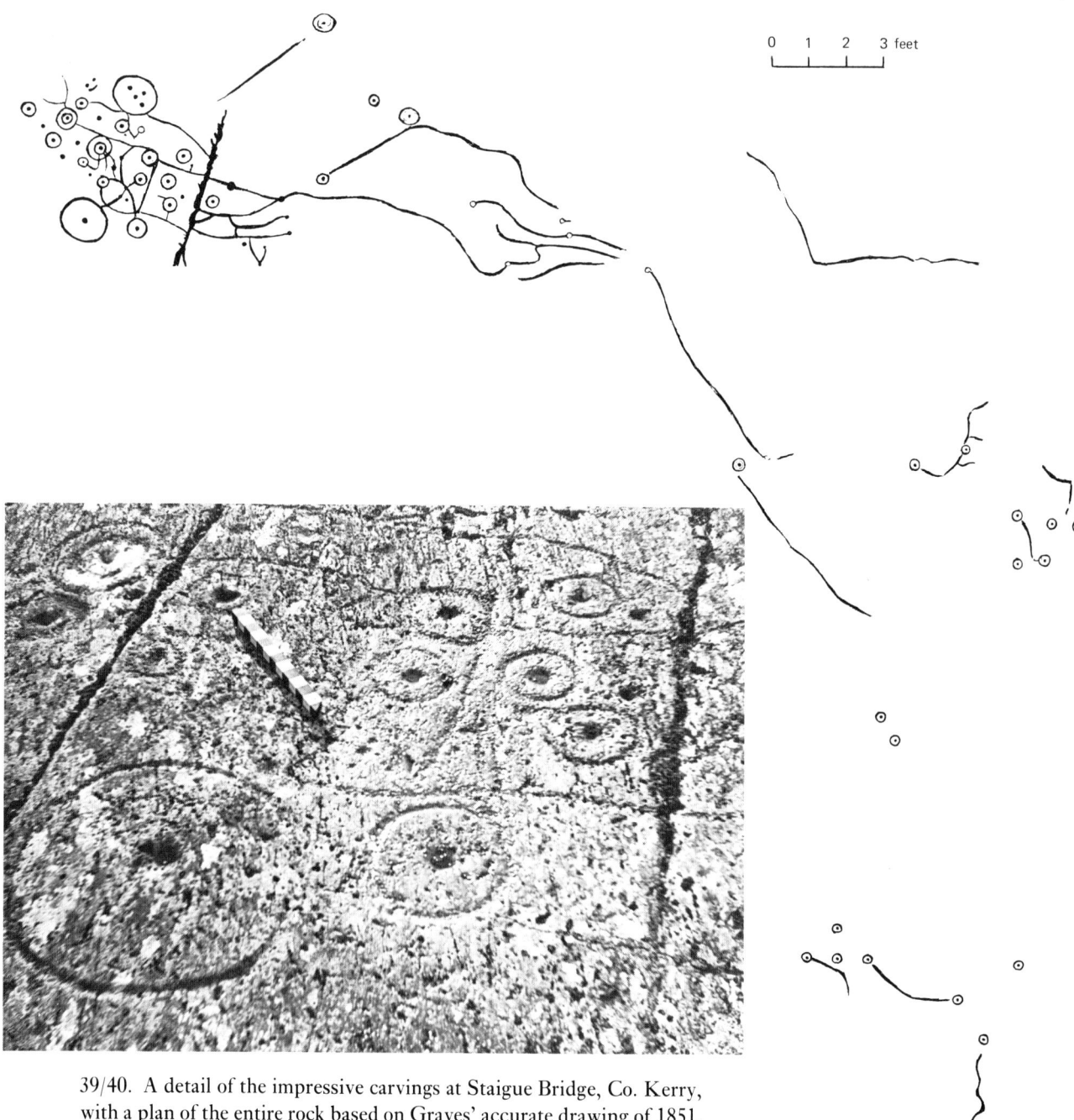

39/40. A detail of the impressive carvings at Staigue Bridge, Co. Kerry,
with a plan of the entire rock based on Graves' accurate drawing of 1851.

Reverend William Greenwell in Northumberland, looked for an   29
explanation of the curious patterns, it was natural to identify the circles
with the outlines of prehistoric forts. They could not have known that
perhaps as much as 2,000 years separated the builders of the defences
and the carvers of the rings. In these circumstances, the Reverend
Graves'

'conjecture that these carvings were primitive maps, representing the disposition of the neighbouring forts'

... was a logical guess and Greenwell made similar suggestions. Since Greenwell noted that barrows were frequently found not far from the Northumberland carvings, it struck him

'that the markings on a rock might be a sort of index to the interments belonging to the tribe within whose territory the rock was situated. That a hollow denoted one burial, say in a tumulus, a circle around it a second burial, and so on . . .'

The first note of disagreement with such easy solutions of the cup-and-ring problem was sounded in a classic study of the Northumberland carvings published in 1865. Its author, George Tate, argued that the carvings were 'symbolic figures, representing religious thoughts' and explained,

'I cannot regard them as the amusements of an idle soldiery, nor as plans of camps, nor as exercises of incipient engineers; for their wide distribution, and notwithstanding differences in detail, their family resemblance prove that they had a common origin, and indicate a symbolic meaning representing some popular thought . . .'

Tate's observation presents the cup-and-ring mystery in its simplest terms. Despite local variations and exceptional carvings in each region, it is difficult to resist the idea that a common convention lies behind patterns in areas as widely separated as Kerry, Aberdeen and Yorkshire, a surprisingly rigid convention with a much more limited range of symbols than that of passage grave art. It is a small step to imagine that the symbols must also have a limited meaning, perhaps even one solution, and this accounts for the attempts of so many investigators to 'decode' the cup-and-ring carvings.

The Speculators

In his definitive 1969 study of the southern Scottish group, Ronald W. B. Morris summarized some 25 different theories (including ten

'more or less fanciful . . . adder lairs, knife-sharpening holes, moulds for metals, sex-rites, masonic marks, grinding mills, anvil-stones, lamps, early writings, and the druids')

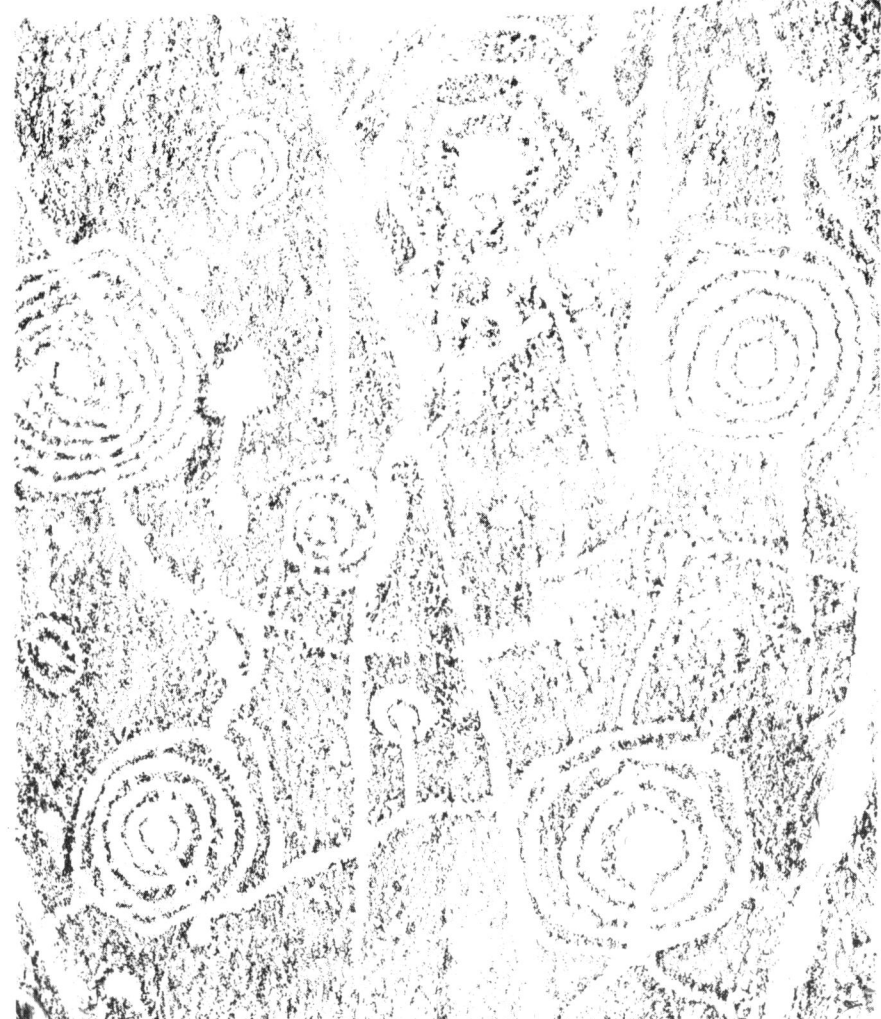

41. An arrangement of fiv
large rings at Achnabreck
Argyll. The width of th
rubbing is about 58 ins (14
cm).

all seeking to explain the purpose of the carvings. Some of the more popular explanations serve to show the wide range of possibilities. For example, a common suggestion was that the cup-and-ring rocks were sacrificial or augury stones, and that the radial groove which so often runs outward from the central cup was a 'gutter' for the blood or liquid involved. While in general the grooves *do* run down the slope of the rocks, the rule is not invariable; at Torbhlaran, mid-Argyll, they run against the gradient. Moreover the appearance of designs on the vertical faces of standing stones seems to argue against the theory.

A more plausible suggestion, advanced some years ago by Professor Stuart Piggott and others, is that the designs represent the magical signs of the earliest metal prospectors in their search for ore-bearing

30

46

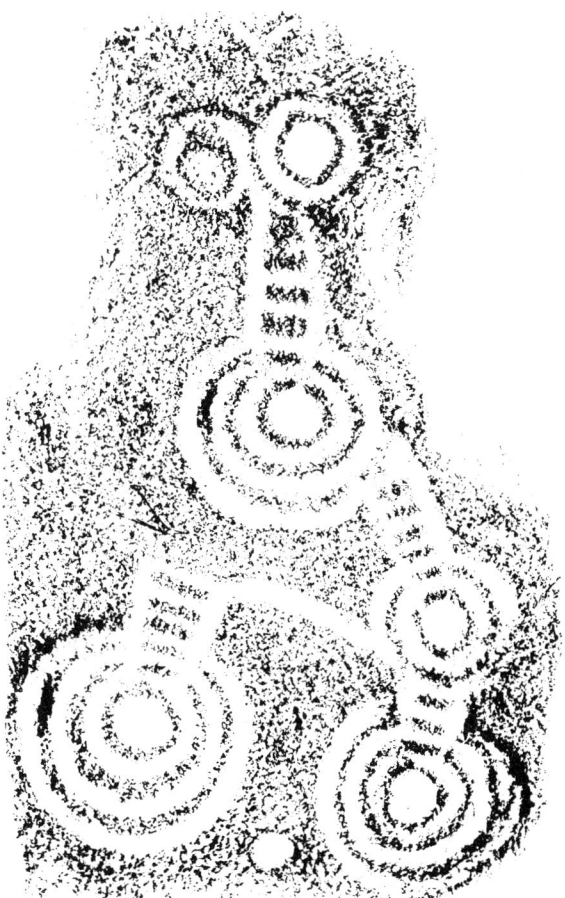

42. A detail from one corner of the Panorama Stone, Ilkley Moor. Maximum width of rubbing is about $28\frac{1}{2}$ ins (72 cm).

rocks. This theory envisages the introduction of the carvings some time around 2000 BC and a close correspondence between the location of the carvings and deposits of copper and gold. A number of local studies seemed to confirm the thesis. For example, the important concentration of carvings in the Strath Tay valley in eastern Scotland is situated close to copper and gold resources by Loch Tay. The analysis of the southern Scottish group by Morris showed that about 84 per cent of fixed rock surfaces were located near copper or gold. This impressive figure, however, does not indicate an even distribution throughout the area, since in the south-eastern district the proportion is only 65 per cent and the overall figures drop considerably when the 'moveable' rocks are taken into account. Carvings are known from areas of southern Scotland and south-western Ireland where no copper or gold ores have ever been known. The regions of thick concentration of cup-and-ring rocks—such as the Killarney 'lakes' or the Whithorn peninsula—are among the most temperate and favourable farming and route centres which

31

must have attracted a settled population from early times, and this point provides a more convincing explanation for the distribution of the carvings than the metal-working theory.

Another popular idea is that the cups and rings were executed to record astronomical observations or symbolize beliefs about the sun, moon and stars. Even in the last century, Nathan Heywood had suggested that the 'ladder' patterns on the Ilkley Panorama Rocks

> 'may have been intended as emblematical of some mysterious connection of the earth with the heavens or planets . . . the cups and rings represented planets, and the circles were added to give those planets the appearance of being in motion . . . I venture to suggest that the sculpturings have been used as diagrams either by astrologers or worshippers of the stars or planets, or both.'

In 1915 L. M. Mann wrote a bizarre paper on *Archaic Sculpturings* which proposed that the rings represented celestial bodies orbiting round a 'Supreme Central Force', supposedly worshipped over most of prehistoric Europe. Then in a book on the monuments of Aberdeenshire published in 1921, G. F. Browne drew attention to the dozens of simple cup-marks found on the large recumbent slabs which are a special feature of the stone circles in the area. At the Sunhoney circle, for instance, he claimed that a pattern of cups represented the constellations of Hercules, Corona, the Little and Great Bear, arranged in their proper respective positions. This was an

> 'instruction chart on which the magician could teach his apprentice, instead of teaching him by pointing with his finger to the stars in the sky.'

At the Rothiemay site, the 107 cups, eight of them surrounded by a single ring, were interpreted as a *reversed* star chart, including the positions of the Pole and seven first magnitude stars, for the convenience of neighbouring magicians who could print off their own copies onto skins with some kind of adhesive colouring material.

A less frivolous suggestion was made in a paper by Professor Alexander Thom in 1966, who pointed out that a complex carving on an outlying boulder close to the Monzie monument in Perthshire coincided with a rough stellar alignment from the centre of the cairn. Cup-marked boulders placed in astronomically significant positions have been noted from the Clava cairns, Inverness, and from the stone rings at

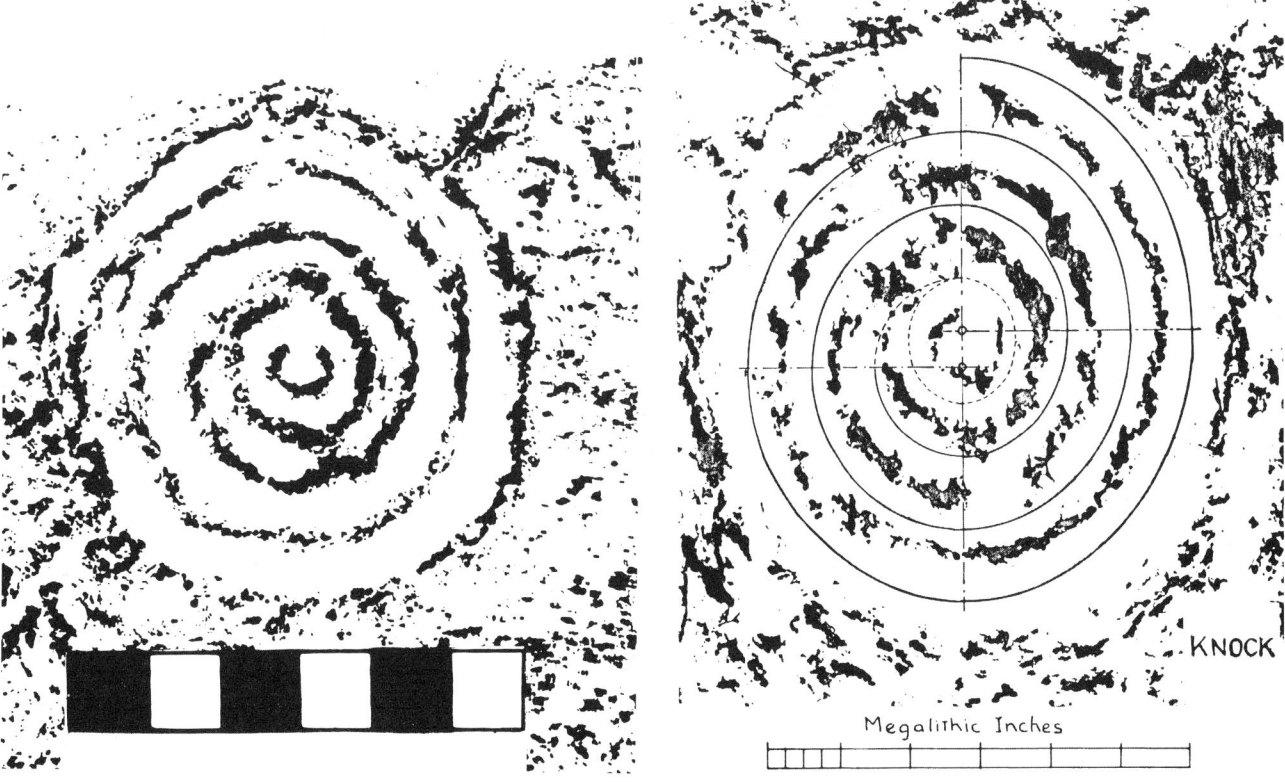

KNOCK

Megalithic Inches

43. The author's rubbing of the spiral at Knock, Wigtownshire, beside a similar rubbing by Mr R. W. B. Morris, with a construction of half-ellipses superimposed by Professor A. Thom. The two rubbings are *not* reproduced at an identical scale; the scale on the left is in inches.

Er-Lannic, Brittany. However, all these are exceptional sites and the astronomical alignment is not well-defined at any of them. If the carvings are an astronomical code, their complete absence from the few unambiguously astronomical sites (such as Callanish or Ballochroy) needs to be explained. As Reverend Graves mentioned over a century ago, 32 33

'In astronomical diagrams, one could hardly fail to recognize a single symbol conspicuous among the rest as denoting the sun or moon, or two such symbols denoting both these bodies. One might also expect to see some delineation, even by the rudest hand, of the phases of the moon. We look in vain for these indications of an astronomical reference in the groups of lines and circles . . .'

An extension of the semi-scientific argument has been developed by Professor Thom in two studies of the geometry of cup-and-ring marks. In over thirty years of survey and investigation of the megalithic monuments of Britain, Thom has shown that a large number of the sites are not circular at all, but are set out so that the stones form regularly distorted patterns, including ellipses and egg-shapes. His work also presents evidence for the existence of a standard unit of length (the megalithic yard of 2·72 feet) that was employed in the construction of monuments from northern Scoltand to southern Brittany. Thom examined wax rubbings of sixty circular designs and calculated that a standard unit of 0·816 inches, or one fortieth of a megalithic yard (the 'megalithic inch') was present in their design. From this basis he examined a number of non-circular patterns (including spirals, triangles, 'ellipses' and 'egg-shapes') 1nd demonstrated that the carvings followed the same conditions that governed the layout of megalithic monuments. The results seemed to show that a few carvings were carefully proportioned designs, involving the use of a number of unusual Pythagorean triangles in their preparation.

These papers deserve careful study, although they involve much wider questions about the validity of megalithic measurements which are still being argued by many statisticians. Clearly any doubt cast on the existence of the megalithic yard affects our acceptance of the megalithic inch. A more fundamental point is the poor accuracy of the

44. Two cups and rings at Achnabreck, Argyll.

wax technique for recording the carvings. While rubbing often shows the designs to best advantage especially if the rock is badly weathered, the method only results in a 'negative' that may give a false impression of regularity to the carved areas. Professor Thom's theory needs to be tested on carvings recorded by a direct tracing method (such as the polythene sheet technique developed by Cork University). At a large concentration like Achnabreck, the presence of so many irregular cups and rings side-by-side with a few more proficiently executed designs makes one wonder if *all* the patterns could not have been achieved by eye alone. The smoothing of the basic pocked designs both by the original carvers and by the forces of erosion is a factor which makes the initial precision of the pattern difficult to assess. The imposition of geometry on the carvings may prove to be as subjective an approach as the constellation theory.

The shortcomings of each one of these comprehensive solutions to the cup-and-ring problem suggest that such an approach may be entirely on the wrong track. First we need to examine the roots of the problem to understand why a simple answer will not work.

Where the Carvings are Found

1: *On natural rock slabs and boulders*

The most striking fact about cup-and-ring carvings is the almost exclusive appearance of 'complex' designs on horizontal rock outcrops. 'Complex' here refers to designs which include more than simple cup-mark depressions or single encircling rings. The general absence of complicated patterns from the other objects commonly selected for carving—such as small boulders and standing stones—may partly be a question of the technical difficulty of executing the designs on these surfaces. However, this explanation is not quite sufficient to account for the marked contrast between complex and simple carvings noticeable by any visitor to a large cup-and-ring group. The careful siting of complex patterns not merely on the nearest available flat rock but on impressive slabs which usually overlook wide-ranging views, should excite the visitor's curiosity. Could the peculiarity of the outcrop designs be a reflection of the sacred character of the rocks themselves or of the sites in question?

A number of these observations have been confirmed in studies of particular regional areas. Throughout southern Scotland, the majority 35 of carvings are found below 400 feet and within a mile or two of the sea.

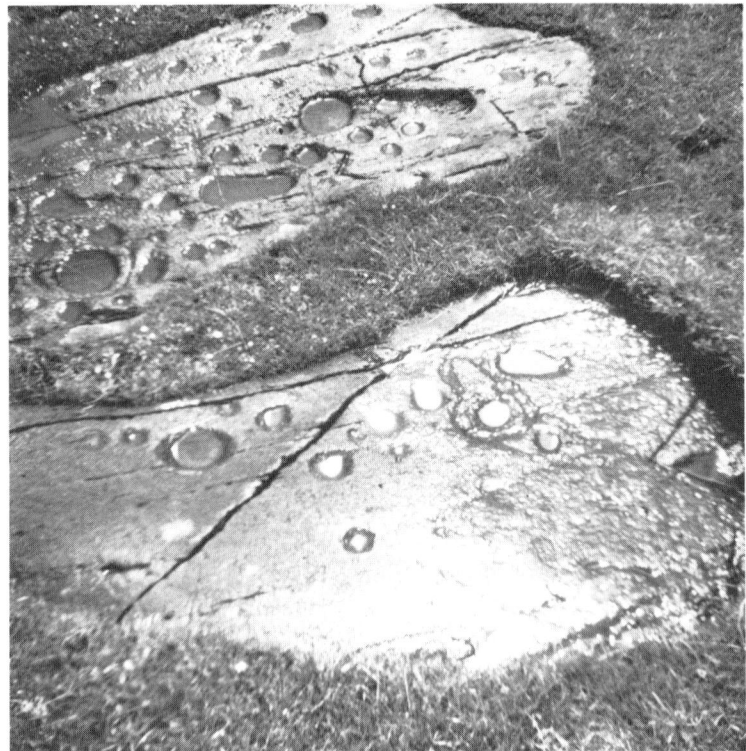

45. Weathered cup and 'keyhole' patterns at Kilmichael Glassary, Argyll.

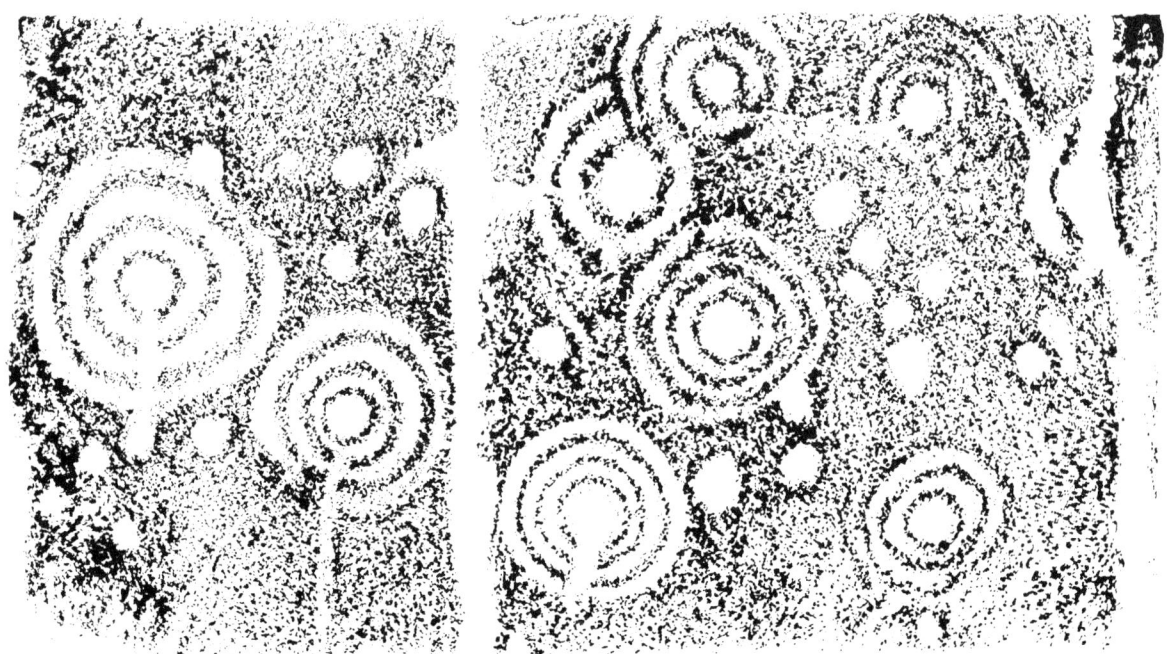

46. A rubbing of the stone at Torbhlaran, Argyll. Note the superimposed rings at the top of the rubbing. Approximate width of rubbing 60 ins (152 cm).

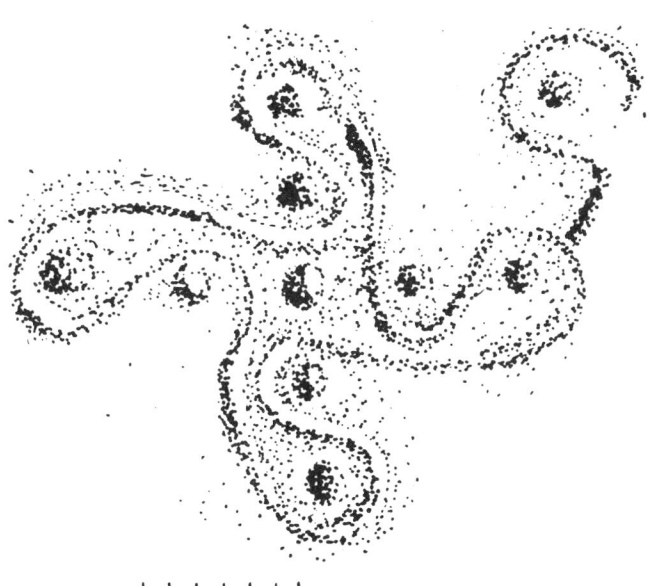

47. The Swastika Stone, Ilkley Moor, based on a photograph. Scale in inches.

It is unusual to find cups and rings at any location far inland, with the exception of the West Yorkshire group. The preference for a horizontal surface is a remarkably consistent factor: it is rare to find any carved area with a slope of more than 20°. The analysis of the Tay Valley region demonstrates clearly the separation of cup-marked boulders on the lower slopes or valley floor and the cups and rings on the outcrops above the 500-foot contour.

In the mid–Argyll district, however, the contrast in styles is apparent at two sites situated on the plain of the River Add. At Kilmichael Glassary, a natural rock slab is pitted with dozens of crude cup and keyhole carvings, while only a mile further down the valley is the hump-backed Torbhlaran outcrop with its series of delicately worked cups and rings.

The West Yorkshire group is characterized by differences not only within a local concentration of sites, but also between whole moorland areas. For example, cups and multiple rings are known from the flat millstone grit outcrops on the northern and western fringes of Ilkley Moor, with the most complicated patterns clustered high over the modern town of Ilkley. These include some quite exceptional carvings such as the Hanging Stones, the Panorama Stone and the famous Swastika Stone with its surprisingly regular pattern, sometimes considered as dating to the Iron Age despite cruder attempts at similar designs on other cup-and-ring surfaces. Yet less than a mile south-west of the Hanging Stones, on the ridge of Green Crag Slack, lie several rocks riddled with simple cup-marks. At the neighbouring moors of Baildon

48/9. This stone, originally flat, is typical of the rough cup-marked boulders of the Baildon Moor group, here contrasted with one of the intricate patterns on the Hanging Stones overlooking Ilkley (*right*). The two sites are about three miles apart.

and Snowden, this type of carving predominates, with the cups sometimes circled or joined by wandering lines, and appears on insignificant looking flat boulders almost lost in the surrounding grass. The overall contrasts between Ilkley, Baildon and Snowden prompted speculation from local experts on which group was likely to have come first. Such arguments are little more than guesswork when there are no independent clues to assist with the relative dating of the rocks. The West Yorkshire carvings, however, clearly present the possibility that the cups and rings cover a wide period of time and a diversity of styles.

An even more striking regional contrast is present in the Northumberland carvings. Once again, many of the most unusual designs are concentrated within a comparatively small area, on the moorland east and south of Doddington. High up on Dod Law is the slab with irregular multiple squares which suggested the outline of Iron Age ramparts to its earliest investigators. At Fowberry Park there is a curious rectangle seven feet long outlined by well over a hundred 'midget' cup-marks. Further north at Roughting Linn, a rock surface with over sixty carvings, some of them of great size, also displays a few exceptional motifs such as 'boxed' U's and a cup-and-ring with nine rays. About ten miles south of the Doddington area around the valley of the River

36

37

Coquet is another group of rocks of a quite different character. Multiple rings and other complex variations are almost entirely absent, while patterns of plain cup-marks and deep basins are common, particularly at the Lordenshaws camp. Around this site are a series of grooves up to thirty feet long and six inches deep, which in some cases begin at a basin and meander down the slope of the rock to its furthest edge. While some of these extraordinary channels may be the result of natural erosion, their close association with conventional cup-and-ring carvings implies that they once had some special significance.

The suspicion that a massive decorated surface such as Roughting Linn was the work of more than one carver at one time is possibly confirmed at Achnabreck, Argyll, where among the dozens of multiple ring patterns, a few seem to be obliterated by subsequent picking. Unlike Newgrange, this deliberate erasure does not blanket out the whole face of the stone but is confined to the area of the circular design itself. An important early commentator, Romilly Allen, was convinced of the random arrangement of cup-and-ring patterns, suggesting 38

'that they were executed one by one, at different times, either by the same or different individuals . . .'

One of the most remarkable cup-and-ring sites was revealed in the summer of 1973, when turf was stripped from a rock at Ormaig, near Loch Craignish, Argyll. The vegetation had perfectly preserved a mass 39 of cup-marks, some in rosette patterns, and three unique cup and circle motifs, each surrounding a central hollow. When the turf was removed, two objects were discovered on the rock surface, among the very few finds ever to be associated directly with a cup-and-ring carving. These were a small flint graving tool such as might well have been used to outline the basic designs, and a slate disc about a centimetre across which was found lying in a cup. Regrettably there is no way of knowing whether these objects were connected with the original period of the carvings or were simply dropped on the site at some later time. However, aside from these tantalizing finds, the significance of the Ormaig rock is again that of an exceptional pattern in a region of more conventional cup-and-ring sites, just in the way that the main Derrynablaha and Dod Law stones stand out among the Kerry and Northumberland groups. These unique designs demonstrate that we are not investigating a single code with a functional explanation, but a complex symbolic practice with a magical or mystical dimension that can only be left to our imagination.

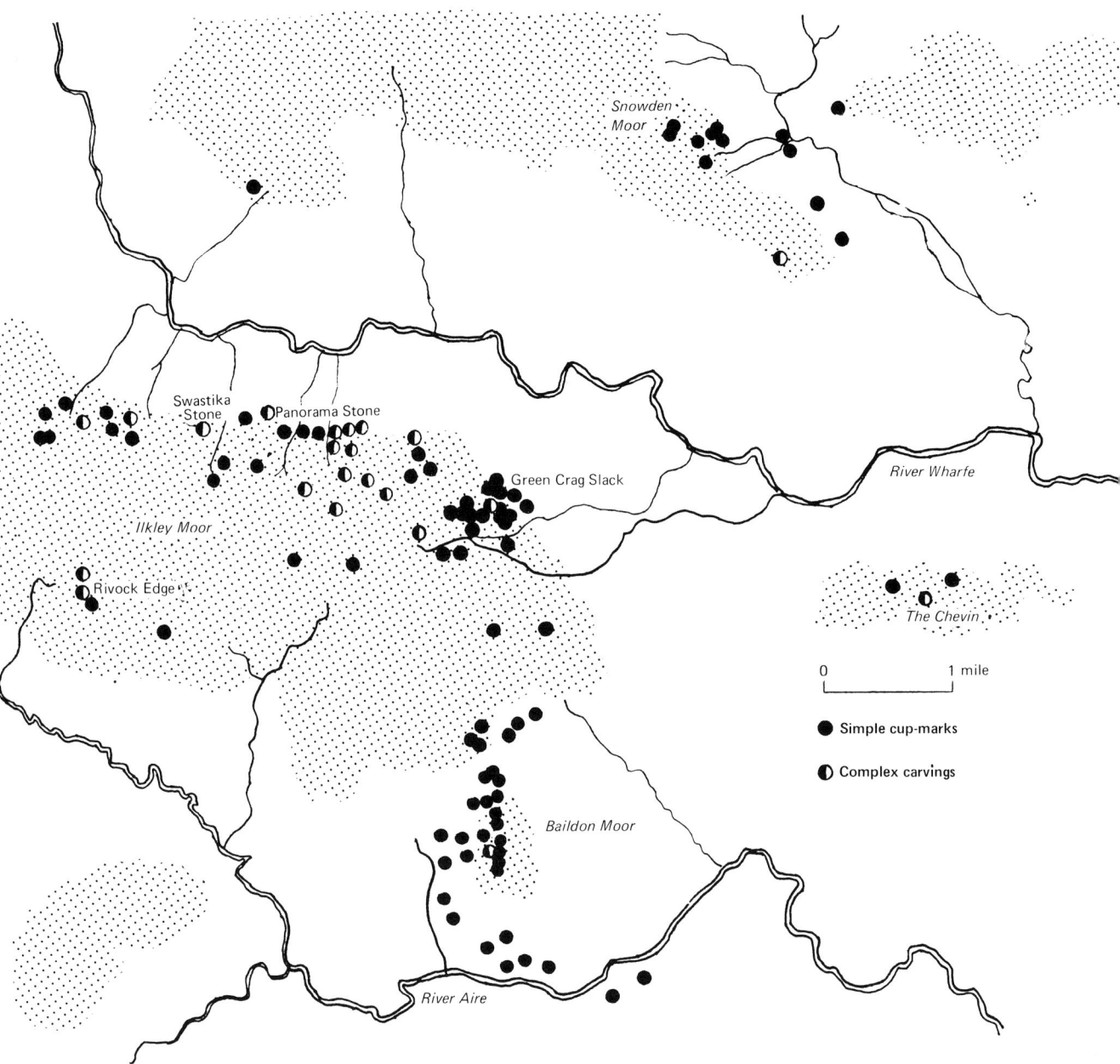

Snowden Moor

River Wharfe

Swastika Stone

Panorama Stone

Green Crag Slack

Ilkley Moor

The Chevin

Rivock Edge

0   1 mile

● Simple cup-marks

◐ Complex carvings

Baildon Moor

River Aire

50/1. Maps of the West Yorkshire (*above*) and Northumberland (*right*) cup-and-ring groups, showing the separation between areas of simple cup-marking and centres of more complicated designs.

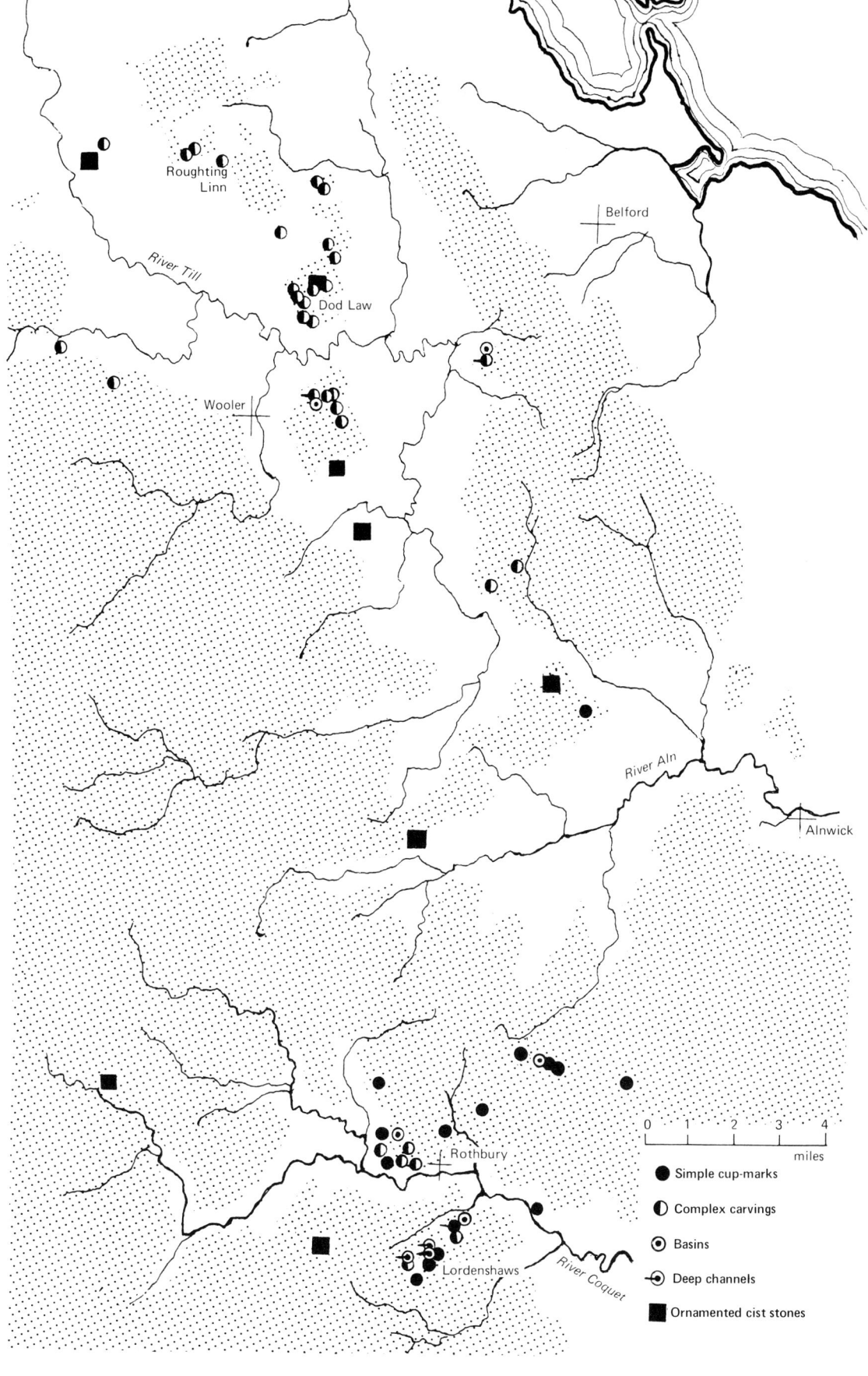

Roughting
Linn

River Till

Belford

Dod Law

Wooler

River Aln

Alnwick

Rothbury

Lordenshaws

River Coquet

0   1   2   3   4
miles

● Simple cup-marks

◑ Complex carvings

◉ Basins

◔ Deep channels

■ Ornamented cist stones

52. Detail of a large decorated rock on Weetwood Moor, Northumberland.

53. This strange pattern of over 100 midget cup-marks (chalked in) is found alongside cup-and-ring carvings at Fowberry Park, Northumberland.

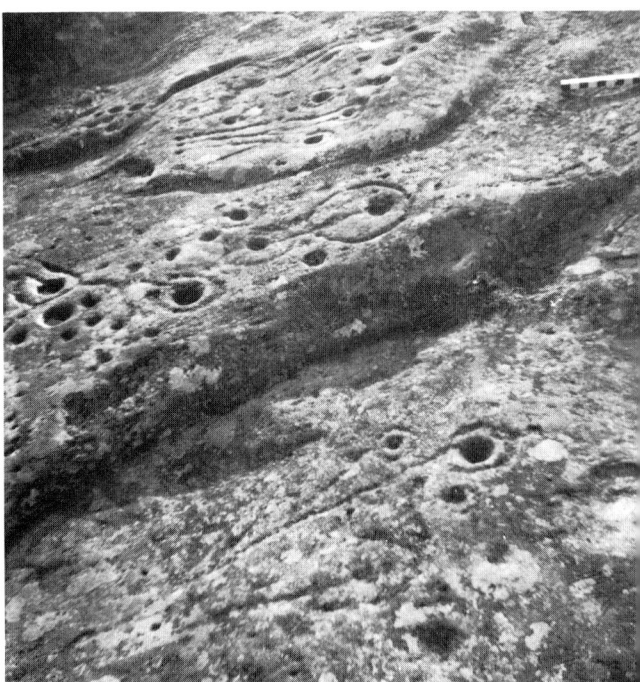

54/5. Two views of England's most impressive carving site at Roughting Linn, Northumberland.

56. A highly unusual U-shaped motif at Roughting Linn, Northumberland.

57/8. At Lordenshaws, Northumberland, deep basins and channels (some of which are probably of natural geological origin) are closely associated with cup-and-ring carvings. The great channel (*above*) begins at a basin, runs down the rock for 30 feet and is about 6 inches deep. Another remarkable rock (*below*) features midget cups and basins, some of which are surrounded by a single ring.

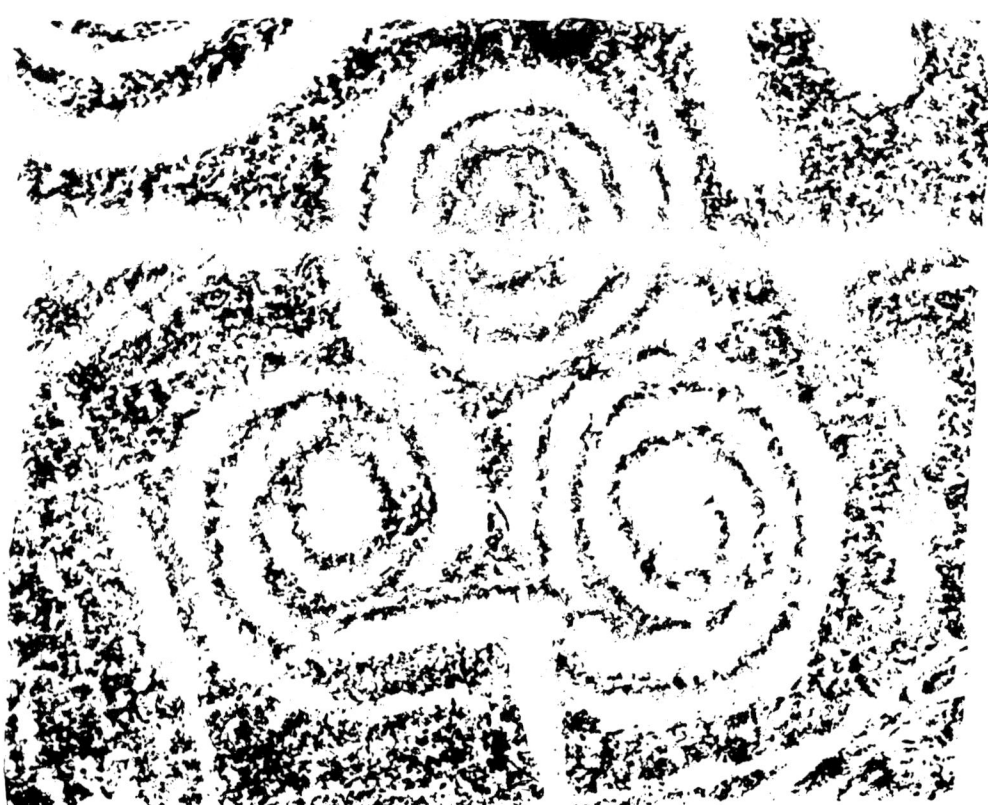

59. A rare cup-and-ring motif at Ormaig, Argyll. Width of largest ring about 12 ins (31 cm).

60. The Achnabreck 'clover leaf' design. Width of rubbing 19½ ins (50 cm).

2: *On chambered tombs, c.* 4000–2000 *BC*

Simple cup-markings appear to have been the oldest and most enduring element in the carving tradition, and from the beginning they were associated with burial monuments. Among the earliest types are the long barrows of southern and eastern England, some of which reflect collective burial customs as long ago as 3400 BC, when extensive clearance of woodland by Neolithic herdsmen and cultivators had already taken place. Recent fieldwork has added some fifty long mounds from Scotland to the well-known sites in the south, and excavation of the Dalladies barrow, Perthshire, has greatly increased our knowledge of these monuments. The excavations confirmed, for example, that long barrows frequently cover several phases of construction and re-use, involving wooden and stone rectangular 'houses for the dead'. At Dalladies the mortuary structure had been reconstructed once and finally burnt after the burials and grave goods had been removed and before

40

41. One of the fragments of carving from the Traprain Law site, Midlothian, now destroyed by quarrying. The pieces are covered with scratched or incised cups and rings and curious grid-like patterns; in one section, roughly pocked lines and circles overlie the incised ornament.

the entire area was covered over by the long mound. The burning of the second structure at Dalladies has been dated to about 3200 BC by the radiocarbon method, and on the floor was discovered a fine flint knife and a boulder with eight cup-marks, lying face up over a post-hole of the previous building. Since the entire mortuary site was covered by the long barrow, the cups are probably not later than the rough dating of 3200 BC.

Although no other long barrow carvings have so far been found, there are a few cup-marked stones known among the hundreds of chambered tombs scattered along the major coastal and island regions of Wales and Scotland. These monuments represent a rich and complex tradition of megalithic burial, in which the Irish passage graves played one influential part. The dating of many tombs is still a matter of speculation, since the tradition probably flourished for at least 2,000 years from its beginnings in the fourth millennium, each local community developing its own special variations on the collective burial theme. The relative scarcity of cups on these structures may indicate that they are secondary carvings, added to the tombs at a later period. The persistent veneration and re-use of ancient sites is a well-substantiated feature of the Neolithic period. At an impressive chambered tomb at Cairnholy, Kirkcudbright, for example, a cup-and-ring slab was propped up against one side of the small box-like chamber, probably inserted along with a secondary burial some time in the early Bronze Age. If the fundamental ideas which lay behind cup-and-ring carvings originated before 3000 BC, then there also existed a sense of religious continuity which would have enabled the tradition to survive and develop over a millennium or more.

The gradual evolution of several types of related monument in a particular region, with cup-marking as a common feature, has been debated in recent studies of north-east Scotland. The arguments centre around the remarkable group of passage graves at Clava near Inverness, 42 which (except for their circular chambers) are very reminiscent of the classic Irish tombs. However the scarcity of finds from these monuments and the discovery of a single burial at one site opens up a considerable range of possibilities for their dating. Were they the result of a supposed initial 'wave' of European passage grave building, perhaps sometime before 2500 BC, which somehow found its way right round to the Great Glen? Or are they Bronze Age imitations, perhaps built as much as a thousand years later, combining a respect for old architectural forms with new customs of single burial? The question is important, because the age when cup-marking was common in northern Scotland, together with the sequence of a whole range of other related sites, depends on the answer.

The practice of cup-marking was widespread in this distinctive region. Three of the Clava passage graves incorporate cup stones, and the concentration of decorated boulders in the vicinity of the tombs suggests that the original carving was roughly contemporary with their construction. While the inclusion of these cup-marks in the fabric of the tombs and other local monuments (such as the ring-cairns) may be largely fortuitous, a few cases indicate the possible symbolic importance of some of the carvings. For example, the corbelled roof of the Corrimony passage grave featured a final covering slab pitted with cup-marks on its underside, and similar carvings are found facing inwards on the chambers and passages of the Clava tombs. The decorated stone in the kerb of the ring-cairn at Tordarroch is also turned inwards against the rubble where it would never have been seen, which could suggest that the builders had ideas comparable to the purposes of the hidden ornament at Newgrange and Knowth. The very rough orientation of the Clava passages towards the south-west and the midwinter sunset has prompted the theory that the positions of the cup-marked stones were also astronomically significant, but there are difficulties in 43 substantiating this from an entirely theoretical observation point in the centre of the chambers or of the cairns. The Clava tombs *do* clearly

62

confirm the connection between cup-marking and the rites of the dead, and further evidence of their precise age or origin may some day throw important light on the carving tradition.

3: *On stones in single graves, c.* 2000–1400 *BC*

Settlers from the middle and delta areas of the Rhine arrived in Britain from about 2000 BC, bringing with them a distinctive type of flat-bottomed, decorated pottery vessel or beaker, together with their custom of single burial under round barrows. The available evidence seems to show that the existing population peacefully absorbed these new influences. From the numerous depositions of beakers in chambered tombs it is clear that the single grave people retained a respect for the

62. A remarkable perforated cist cover from Redbrae, Wigtownshire. Note the incised lines and the rough lozenge pattern above the hole. Width approximately 23 ins (59 cm).

collective burial traditions of the past. Just as the covering stones of single graves carved with passage grave symbols appear in many cases to be broken-up slabs, so a significant number of the cup-and-ring ornamented graves seem to include re-used stones. Rather than imitate old patterns, the single grave builders evidently preferred to find existing decorated stones and to adapt them to fit in with the structure

of their burial cists.

If the creation of new cup-and-ring stones had ceased before the spread of single grave practices, it may explain why there is such a complete absence of carved stones from these graves in important cup-and-ring districts such as Kerry and Strath Tay. In the Kilmartin valley, Argyll, typical cup-and-ring motifs at Achnabreck, Cairnbaan, Baluachraig or Poltalloch form a complete contrast to the decorated stones inside the cairns of the impressive valley cemetery, with their naturalistic axe carvings (discussed in the next chapter). While the evidence may not be particularly strong, the distribution map of carved cists may confirm the assumption that complex cup-and-ring carving had died out in some western districts by Bronze Age times, but that in eastern areas its influence persisted.

The only monument to incorporate a flat boulder with complex carving is the small 'kerb-cairn' at Monzie, Perthshire, which is closely similar to other north-east Scottish sites and is distantly related to the cairns and tombs of Clava. Cup-marking and the scattering of white quartz fragments seem to be characteristic of the ritual at this group of sites. A flat boulder with simple cup-marking was built into the kerb of a small kerb-cairn at Balnuaran, which surrounded a shallow burial pit with a concentration of quartz at one end. At Culcharron, Argyll, the cup-marked stone lay just outside the kerb of the cairn, while at the Croft Moraig stone circle, Perthshire, the axis of the second phase of the monument ran south-west through a cup-marked slab built into the enclosing stone bank. All these sites seem connected, perhaps coincidentally, by the occurrence of quartz, of flat decorated stones and of standing stones carefully graded in height. Perhaps these stones might

44

45
46

47

63. Part of the well-preserv cup-and-ring rock at Polt: loch, Argyll. Approxima width of rubbing 32 ins (cm).

64

give us some clue to the age when carving on other horizontal boulders and outcrops was practised, but unfortunately the range of dates is again too vague for any useful speculation. It is obvious, however, that in the late Neolithic and early Bronze Age period, the involvement of carved stones with burial and ritual in north-eastern Scotland was particularly close.

Cup-marked stones have been discovered in the rubble and kerb rings of cairns not only in the northern counties but also at a few round barrows scattered through south Wales and south-west England. One of the best known cases is the Tregulland Burrow, Cornwall, where some 21 cup-marked slabs were scattered among the ring of stones beneath the barrow. Such sites confirm that simple cup-marking was a much more widespread and long-lasting practice than the classic cup-and-ring style.

48

4: *On standing stones and stone circles, c.* 2500–1200 *BC*

Probably the best known prehistoric remains in Britain are 'temple' monuments such as Stonehenge, Avebury and Stanton Drew, which consist of circles of large megaliths, sometimes surrounded by an enclosing earthwork. Stone circles have been the subject of study and conjecture for several centuries, and yet it is still difficult to provide generalized explanations of their function and origin. This is due to several factors, notably the small number of properly organized excavations that have taken place at these sites. In any case a large number of the monuments seem to have been kept clear of refuse or occupation material which usually provide the archaeologist with his most helpful clues. It is also apparent that particular regions developed their own special types of stone circle, which sometimes included successive rebuilding phases and perhaps served a variety of functions. An overall contrast exists between monuments of the north and west which frequently surround burial structures, and southern England, where such features are usually absent. Therefore it is unlikely that any one of the conventional theories accounting for the stones, such as ritual gathering places, the 'cult of the dead' or astronomical observatories, will ever successfuly resolve the problems of every megalithic site.

65. The cup-marked central stone from the Kilmartin Stones (Temple Wood) monument, Argyll.

The present range of radiocarbon dates for stone circles covers nearly 2,000 years of prehistory (from the ring around Newgrange— about 2500 BC—to the Perthshire site of Sandy Road which is calculated at roughly 1200 BC). Clearly the megalithic sites are not all that useful in establishing a date for the carvings, particularly in the case of isolated standing stones, where evidence of dating and function is likely to be even harder to discover. Moreover the carvings could have been added some time after the stones were raised. The simple nature of most of the designs, usually confined to cup-marks and simple rings, might be explained by the awkwardness of carving on a vertical surface. However, quite a number of stones have been shown to include cup-marks once below the original ground surface. Other cups are often scattered on only one side of the slab and sometimes as high as 8 or 9 feet from the ground, suggesting that they too were executed before the stone was erected. The question of the simple character of these markings perhaps belongs to the wider issue of why complex patterns were mainly confined to horizontal natural rock surfaces.

An interesting carving came to light in 1973 which confirms that decoration was sometimes completed before a stone was upright. At the Temple Wood circle in Argyll, there is a spiral partly hidden below   49 the packing material around the base of a stone which is due north at the site when seen from the central burial cist. This might well be a re-used slab from some earlier monument.

Cup-marked stone circles are fairly common within the general areas in which cup-and-ring marks are found. One of their most consistent appearances is at monuments in north-east Scotland, at the recumbent stone circles of Aberdeen and its neighbouring counties. Like the Clava passage graves to which these stone circles are related, the positions of the carvings do not seem to be entirely random, but are always concentrated on the recumbent stone itself or on the tall stones immediately to its east and west. The careful grading of the heights of the stones in the circle up to the final flanking pair, draws further attention to the recumbent stone. What was its function? One suggestion is astronomical, since the axis defined by the recumbent stone corresponds to a variety of wintertime solar, lunar and planetary bearings.

The theory envisages observation of the sun, the moon or Venus as it rose or set behind the top of the stone, as seen from the centre of the ring. However, the alignments defined by the recumbent stone are in no case as precise as is sometimes claimed for other types of megalithic site. The recumbent stone circles were clearly never accurate observatories in a modern sense, and so attempts to interpret the cup-markings as a 'code' of observations have proved unconvincing. Perhaps some simpler kind of astronomical meaning or symbolism was involved.

It is tempting to identify the cup-and-ring marks with the circular obsession so apparent in the enclosures, buildings, round barrows and stone circles of late Neolithic times. The distorted figures outlined by some stone circles—whether or not they were set out with a standard unit—reveal a concern with pattern and shape that is surely present at some level in the carvings. Yet the complete absence of cup-and-ring marks from the far north and south of Britain, from great stone circles

66. Rubbing of the spiral discovered at the Temple Wood stone circle in 1973. This shows only the section visible above the packing stones around the base of the megalith. The rubbing is about 12 ins (31 cm) wide.

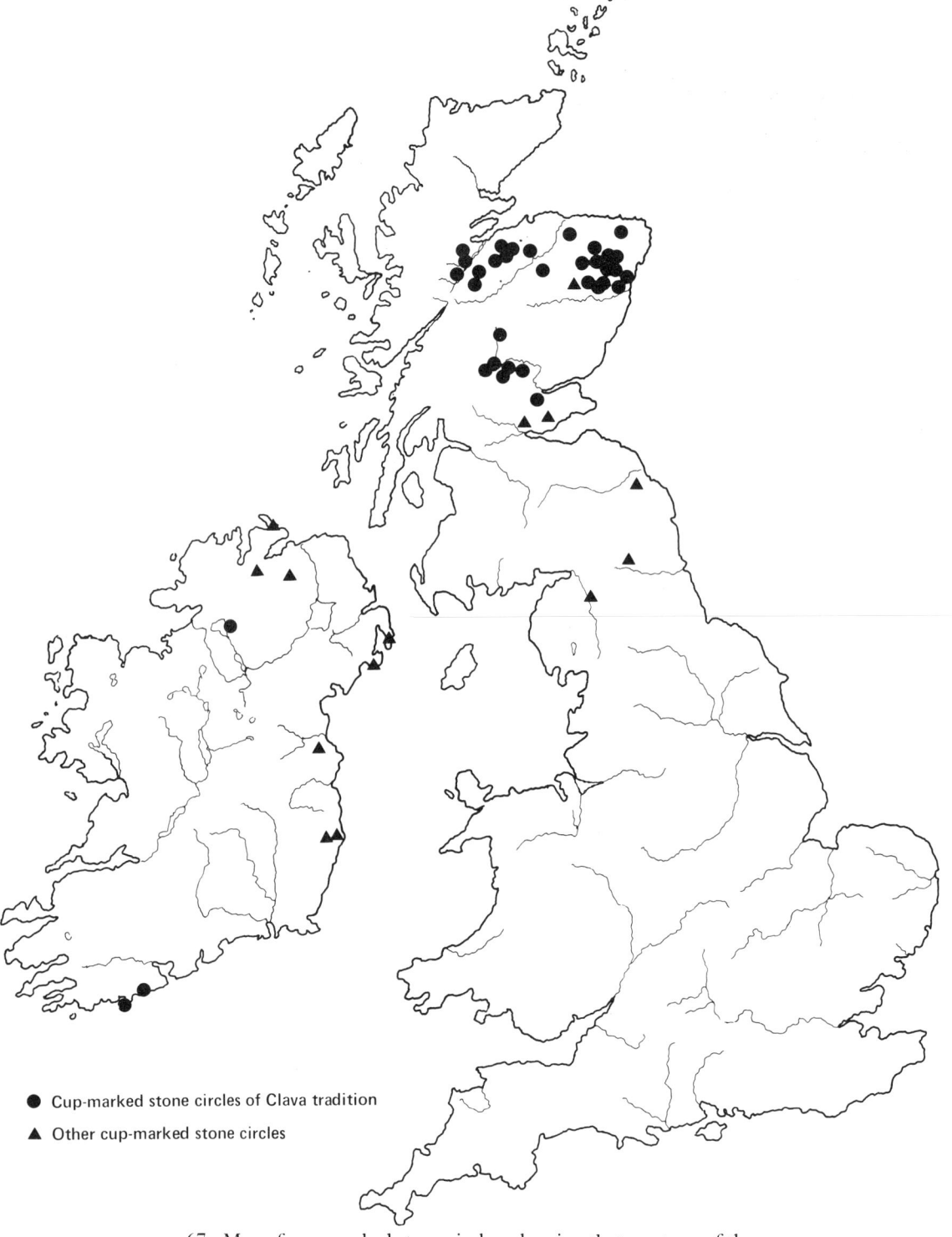

67. Map of cup-marked stone circles, showing that most are of the
Clava type.

● Cup-marked stone circles of Clava tradition

▲ Other cup-marked stone circles

such as Callanish, Avebury or the Ring of Brogar, shows that the traditions of the carvers were not identical to those of the megalith builders. Faced by monuments as impressive as Long Meg or Achnabreck, it is scarcely surprising that many people are convinced by sweeping claims that a unified system of science and religion flourished in prehistoric times. The carvings do show that widely separated communities could share the same symbols and probably the same beliefs, but they also indicate the variety of individual traditions in early Britain. We have already seen that passage grave art motifs seem to have been widely distributed over Britain sometime after 2500 BC, while a conventional guess about the age of cup-and-ring carvings would fall into a similar period. Why did these two traditions remain distinct? Why did the carvers of Derrynablaha or Roughting Linn apparently never feel the urge to pock out a triple spiral or a row of chevrons?

The Two Traditions

The carvings on the outcrops and boulders seem to have called for a narrower selection of symbols than the ornament in the tombs. Did the cups and rings of Kerry and Kirkcudbright develop *from* the art tradition of cemeteries like Loughcrew, or did they precede and perhaps give rise to it?

The separation of the cup-and-ring style from passage grave art is apparent enough in Ireland. Except for the isolated Clear Island stone, no examples of passage grave art are known anywhere near the thickest cup-and-ring concentrations in West Cork and Kerry. No spirals exist in the south-west Irish group. Unbroken concentric rings are the commonest motif, while a further distinctive feature is the frequency of irregular networks of criss-cross lines, interspersed with cups, usually adjoining a conventional cup-and-ring pattern. Radial channels or 'gutters' are quite unusual in Cork and Kerry, but a few spectacular examples—such as on Lake Coomasaharn II or Derrynablaha 10—are closely comparable to motifs at any English or Scottish group.

The distribution of the two styles is not entirely exclusive however, since in County Wicklow there is some overlap between a few cup-and-ring stones and an equally small number of decorated passage graves. A recent discovery of a large carved slab in a field at Ballinvally, County Meath, includes concentric circles broken by radial grooves, and is perhaps closest to the cup-and-ring style. An even more remarkable find came from a fence near the Loughcrew cairns, where a boulder

51

68/9. Cup-marks with branching lines and channels from Lordenshaws, Northumberland (*above*) and Lake Coomasaharn, Co. Kerry (*below*). Are such resemblances the result of chance, or did a common idea inspire carvers in both areas?

70/1. Contrasting patterns from the important Irish cup-and-ring site at Derrynablaha, Co. Kerry. The two rocks (numbered 12 and 10) are only a short distance apart on the same hillside.

72. Part of the carved boulder near the Gates of Glory standing stones, Milltown, Co. Kerry.

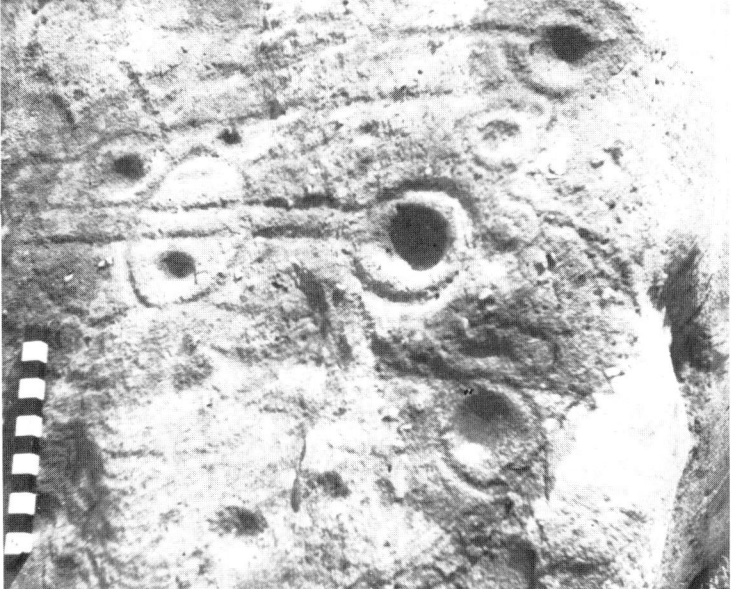

73/4. Were the 'passage grave style' and the 'cup-and-ring style' ever really distinct? The boulder found near the Lough-crew tombs (*left*) has a cup and rings beside a lozenge motif. The decoration in the Tara passage grave (*below*) would not be out of place on a cup-and-ring rock in Kerry.

built into the wall featured 'passage grave' lozenges beside a cup with four rings and a radial groove.

And what of the carvings inside the tombs? As mentioned previously, concentric circles are the most common design outside the Boyne, and examples at Tara and Loughcrew would not be out of place on any cup-and-ring rock in south-west Ireland. It is even possible to trace a rare motif, the Ormaig pattern of a circle of cups, not only on cup-and-ring stones (at Auchenlarie, Kirkcudbright, Carrickrobin, County Louth, and Derrynablaha, Kerry) but also at the Loughcrew cemetery, on a passage upright inside Cairn T, which includes a comparable double ring of cups. Concentric circles appear in the 'hidden' ornament 52 at Newgrange, notably a dot and four rings about a foot across on a corbel covered by the third roofslab of the passage. We can argue, then, that in 2500 BC the carver of the Newgrange corbel was invoking an already established cup-and-ring tradition, which for some reason was considered inappropriate or distinct from the main ornament of the tomb.

If it can be substantiated, this conclusion has remarkable implications. The cup-and-ring rocks of Wigtown and Kirkcudbright and the passage graves of the Boyne are only about a hundred miles apart, and much more direct crossings of the Irish Sea were possible further to the north. There is abundant evidence of contact and trade between the two coastlines throughout the Neolithic period, with strong influences from Ireland evident in the construction of chambered tombs and in the distribution of stone axes. If there is a possibility that the cup-and-ring rocks and the passage grave stones are roughly contemporary, perhaps carved over a period of centuries during the third millennium, then the basic differences between the styles become all the more intriguing.

Some support for this general argument comes from the Wigtown– 53 Kirkcudbright region. Here is found not only the carving group closest to Ireland, but also one of the most dense concentrations of cup-and-ring sites anywhere in Britain, with a large number of unusual patterns. Six spirals are known, notably a magnificent example about two feet across and with seven turns, carved on a block of whinstone at the desolate valley cemetery of Cauldside Burn. The western distribution of the remaining English and Scottish spirals, at sites such as Long Meg, Blackshaw, Achnabreck and Temple Wood could well be ascribed to Boyne influence. It is easy to imagine the south-west Scottish coastal region as a key area where impulses from Ireland were transformed into a vigorous and independent tradition of cup-and-ring carving.

75. The impressive spiral carved on a block of whinstone in the valley cemetery of Cauldside Burn, Kirkcudbright. Maximum width of spiral about $23\frac{1}{2}$ ins (60 cm).

If the origins of both styles can be traced back well before the Bronze Age, it may help to explain the peculiar nature of the designs on single grave slabs, especially in the east of Britain. Many of these cist stones, as we have seen, are probably re-used from an earlier period. A small number also present a mixture of cup-and-ring and passage grave styles which might be thought to date from the Bronze Age when distinctions were breaking down. It was previously noted that cist stones in the passage grave style carry a very restricted range of symbols, with an emphasis on concentric arcs and circles, which might equally be due to a late and mixed tradition.

However, it would be wrong to oversimplify and attempt to answer every question of style with a single solution. The most essential and exciting point is the growing evidence that the lozenges, spirals, cups and circles of Britain may represent the first major west European art tradition in stone since the Ice Age.

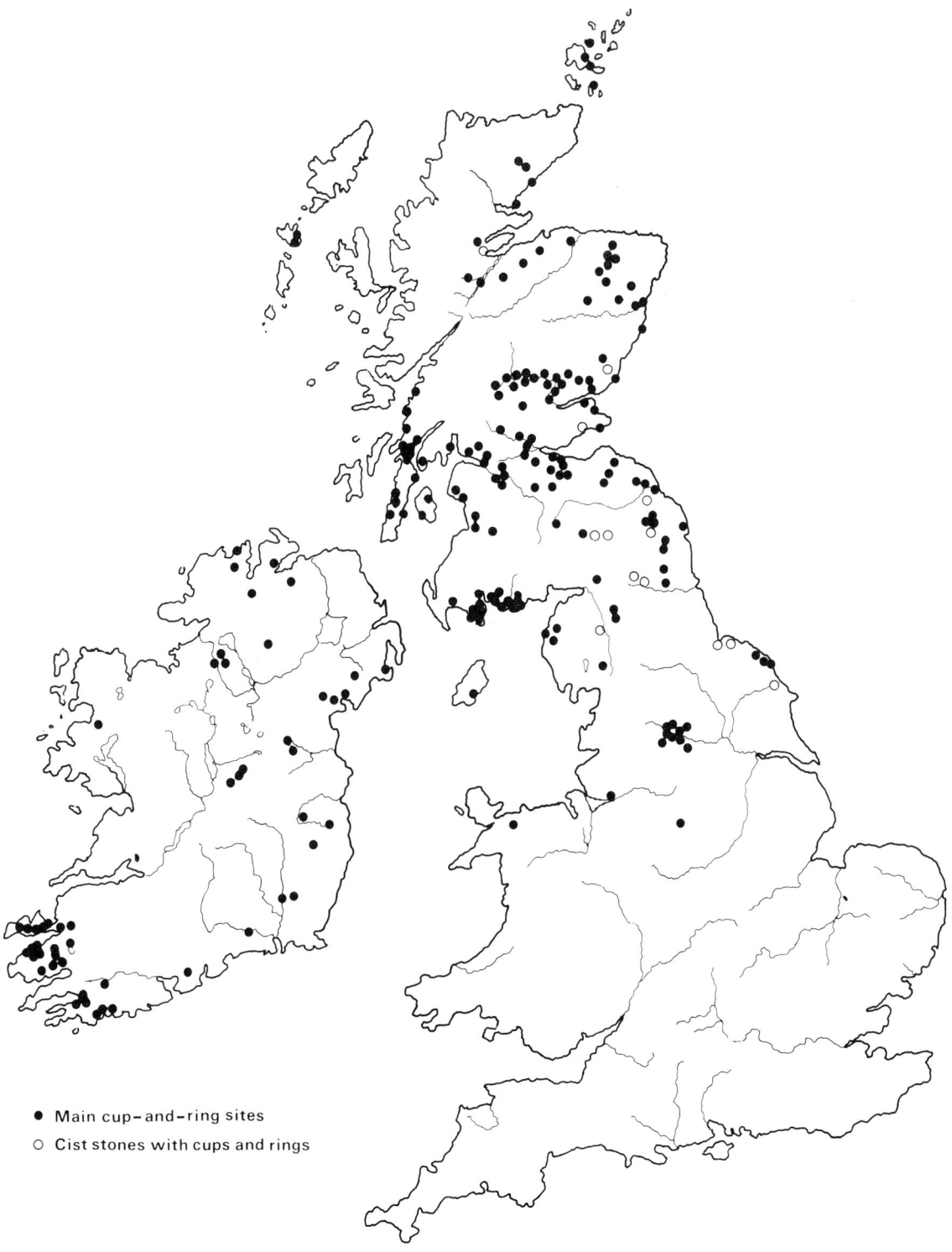

76. Map of the principal cup-and-ring sites.

● Main cup-and-ring sites
○ Cist stones with cups and rings

77. View of the highest part of the main Achnabreck rock showing the double spiral and 'clover leaf' patterns.

78. The largest of dozens of rings at Achnabreck, Argyll. Width of rubbing about 30 ins (76 cm).

The Source of the Carvings

In a sloping field just behind the parish church at Clonfinlough, County Offaly, lies a remarkable slab of limestone. The rock is covered with numerous markings of crosses, pits, 'footprints' and curious ovals bisected by straight lines. In 1920 the Clonfinlough stone was the subject of a classic interpretation by the Abbé Henri Breuil, world authority on cave painting, and Professor R. A. S. Macalister, at that time Ireland's leading archaeologist. Breuil visited Macalister in Dublin and showed him photographs of Neolithic wall-paintings recently discovered by him in Spain.

'I suddenly remembered the excellent lithograph of the Clonfinlough stone' Macalister wrote '. . . and taking the volume down   54

79/80. The controversial carved rock at Clonfinlough, Co. Offaly.

from my shelves, I placed it beside the photographs. My visitor at once agreed that there was an identity of style and purpose in the Irish stone and in the Spanish paintings, and that the two were undoubtedly cognate . . .'

Having established the similarity, the inevitable conclusion was drawn that the Clonfinlough stone (like the passage graves and their art) was produced by prehistoric Spanish·immigrants to Ireland. Macalister embroidered his deduction with a lively and fanciful 'reading' of the stone, which was surely

'. . . the oldest record of the kind in Northern Europe of a historical event. The men contemplating the sculptured field are victors in some encounter: before them is the battle-field, printed with the footmarks of the flying foe, strewn with weapons cast away in their flight and with missile stones—or possibly with severed heads.'

But were the 'men', 'footmarks', 'weapons', 'stones', 'heads'—or rather the ovals, pits and crosses—genuine carvings? In 1967 a careful study of the Clonfinlough stone revealed that most of the markings were in fact wholly natural in origin, resulting from chemical action on the limestone caused by rainwater. Some of the lines were formed by 'strike' and 'dip' joints in the structure of the stone created by compres-

81. An impression of the carving at Lombo da Costa, Pontevedra, Portugal. One-metre scale shown.

sion. Indeed only the ovals seemed to be artificially carved, added to the joints to give the appearance of 'stick-men' or perhaps even hafted axes. There is no indication of any kind to show that these additions to the natural marks were made in Neolithic or even prehistoric times. The Clonfinlough stone is an extreme case where a 'diffusionist' argument was based on shaky foundations.

The Abbé was inclined to interpret cup-and-ring and passage grave designs in a similar spirit. No matter how abstract the pattern, how seemingly random its arrangement, the carvings could be explained as a conventionalized human face, ultimately related to the Iberian 'Mother Goddess'. Cups and rings with double radial grooves were explained as human figures, 'where two lines for the legs are given, though often united by various cross-lines'. The Abbé saw double-ringed cups from the Isle of Arran as figures with arms raised above the head, 'like the feminine figures in the Egyptian pre-dynastic tombs and some Spanish rock paintings'.

The first attempt to discuss a foreign origin on a less subjective basis was made in a paper by Eoin MacWhite in 1946. The Galician 55 cup-and-ring rocks of northern Portugal provided MacWhite with some extraordinarily close models for the British series. Here the student of the British carvings will find all the familiar patterns, circles connected with branching lines, enclosures of cupmarks, gapped rings and criss-cross networks. The tight groupings of motifs often cover expansive areas of flat rock outcrops and make these Portuguese carvings

78

even more impressive than some of the most elaborate British rocks. Sites such as Lambo da Costa or As Tenxiñas might be a plausible starting point for the impulse which led to Achnabreck or Roughting Linn. The special situation of the south-west Irish cup-and-ring group made it the obvious link area by which the tradition was spread from the Atlantic seaways to the rest of northern Britain. MacWhite accepted a general Bronze Age dating for the series and the whole theory seemed to stand up well to critical examination.

However, our recent knowledge of the third millennium date of the passage graves and the probable early origin of the cup-and-ring rocks raises an important question. Do the Galician cups and rings also go back as far as 2500 BC or earlier? Quite a number of them are found alongside carvings of metal axes and daggers, which of course could be later additions. Yet a few of the axeheads depicted on the rocks have expanded ends which are closer to northern European types than to native Bronze Age products. Isolated finds of other objects such as swords, maceheads and golden ornaments also suggest a degree of influence from northern sources. There is a distinct possibility, then, that cup-and-ring marks could have been introduced to the area from Ireland, rather than the other way round. A further point is that the Galician carvings are frequently accompanied by stylized deer outlined in profile, which are clearly derived from the very ancient native Iberian traditions of rock painting. The complete absence of such representational elements in the Irish carvings would be a surprising fact if it was maintained that the cups and rings were introduced by Portuguese trade or settlement.

As far as the present evidence suggests, the British cup-and-ring tradition seems to owe little to outside inspiration. Comparable motifs among the rock art of Scandinavia and burial cists in Germany are confined to a few rare examples. The patterns are found in areas of Europe unlikely to have been directly influenced by contacts with Britain, such as the Swiss Alps, where the recently discovered Carschenna site displays cups and gutters, multiple rings, spirals and wandering lines startlingly like the repertoire of passage grave and cup-and-ring art (but also includes representational figures such as a man on horseback). The appearance of these designs not merely in Europe but all over the world, among ancient traditions as widespread as those of Brazil, India and Australia, indicates the fundamental nature of the impulse to create these simple abstract forms.

Anthropologists and other observers have recorded the significance

56

57

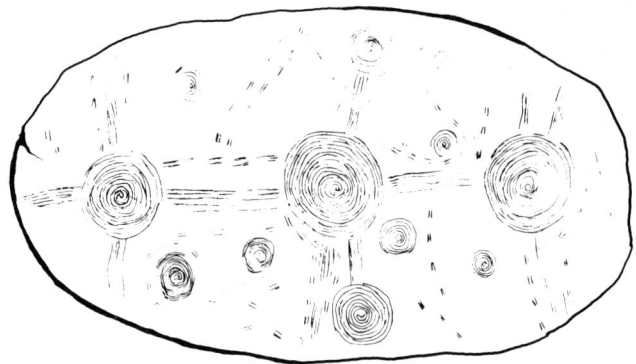

82. Sketch of an Aborigine stone *churinga* or sacred object of the Ngalia, central Australia. Each of the circles represents a place in the story of the grasshopper ancestors of the tribe, whose prints in the sand are shown by the pairs of short lines.

of concentric circles among simple communities of recent times. In some instances, such as the cup-marked rocks of India, the carvings were connected with a specific Hindu cult of generation known as Mahadeo, as a traveller in the last century discovered. 58

'I got a fakir and drew on the sand of the Gogra the figure ⊚. I asked him what that meant. The fakir at once answered, "Mahadeo." I then drew ⊚ and got the same answer. At Delhi my old acquaint- ance, Mr Shaw, told me that these two signs are chalked on stones in Kangra by people marching in marriage processions. The mean- ing given to these two symbols now in India is familiarly known to the people.'

By contrast, the central Australian ground drawings are created as part 59 of elaborate ceremonies re-enacting the descent of a divine ancestor to the earthly world, in which the circles represent the places where the ancestor rested and left his spirit children. The possibility that the symbolic values of cup-and-ring carvings were actively asserted as part of a story 'relived' in periodic ceremonies is an intriguing one. The study of such comparative material can help us to envisage cups and rings through prehistoric eyes, and such an imaginative effort transforms the carvings into something more than remote and abstract patterns. Indeed, to an enthusiast like the Rev. Charles Rogers, steeped in Biblical and Druidical reading, the British carvings evoked the whole spirit of a lost civilization.

'The sculptures are sacred books, which the awe-inspired wor- 60 shipper was required to revere and, probably, to salute with reverence. A single circle represented the sun, two circles in union the sun and moon—Baal and Ashtaroth. The wavy groove passing across the circle pointed to the course of water from the clouds, as discharged upon the earth. Groups of pit marks pointed to the stars or, more probably, to the oaks of the primeval temples.'

3 The Cup and the Cross

The Axe and the Dagger

Within recent times farmers in most north European and Scandinavian countries believed that an ancient axe-head dug up in the fields would bring good luck. The custom of burying such a find in the wall or floor of a house as a protection against evil, and particularly against lightning, was widespread and had very ancient roots. The representational scenes of Scandinavian rock art together with the pagan mythology   61 of the Viking age demonstrate some continuity of belief in the powers of the axe. In the Bronze Age carvings, it is often associated with the dominant sun-disc, and in the legends, with the hammer as the symbol and weapon of the Viking peoples' most popular god, Thor.

Although the evidence is most vividly apparent in the Scandinavian sources, it is equally clear that most north-west European communities considered the axe to be an object of special importance far back into prehistoric times. Stone and flint axes, after all, were the essential tools by which Neolithic farmers and herdsmen cleared forests and established land for agriculture. In Britain the trade in high quality axes spread from a few specialized 'factories' such as Great Langdale in Cumberland and Tievebulliagh in Northern Ireland through every part of the country. The deposition of axes in good condition at ritual monuments such as Avebury, Brogar, Llandegai and elsewhere suggests their special value, if not the use of the monuments as actual trading centres. It is not difficult to imagine the status which the first exploiters of copper and bronze tools must have acquired. The power of such objects is reflected in replicas composed of semi-precious stone which was often traded from far distant sources. For example, several non-functional, 'ceremonial' stone axes from eastern Scotland were fashioned from   62 jadeite which probably came from the Rhineland. In Bronze Age times elaborately carved 'sacred' axeheads, maces and battle-axes were sometimes buried with their owners underneath the round barrows. The huge 'tumulus' monuments of southern Brittany, perhaps   63 of late Neolithic date, often covered particularly elaborate burials, including dozens of stone axes. Many of these were ritually broken in the last rite and were superbly carved and polished from serpentine and jadeite materials, some of which derive from Alpine sources.

With these indications of the special values associated with the axe in Neolithic and Bronze Age times, it is perhaps surprising that no axe carvings appear in the British passage grave and cup-and-ring styles, unless the strange symbol at Knowth is interpreted as one. It is all the

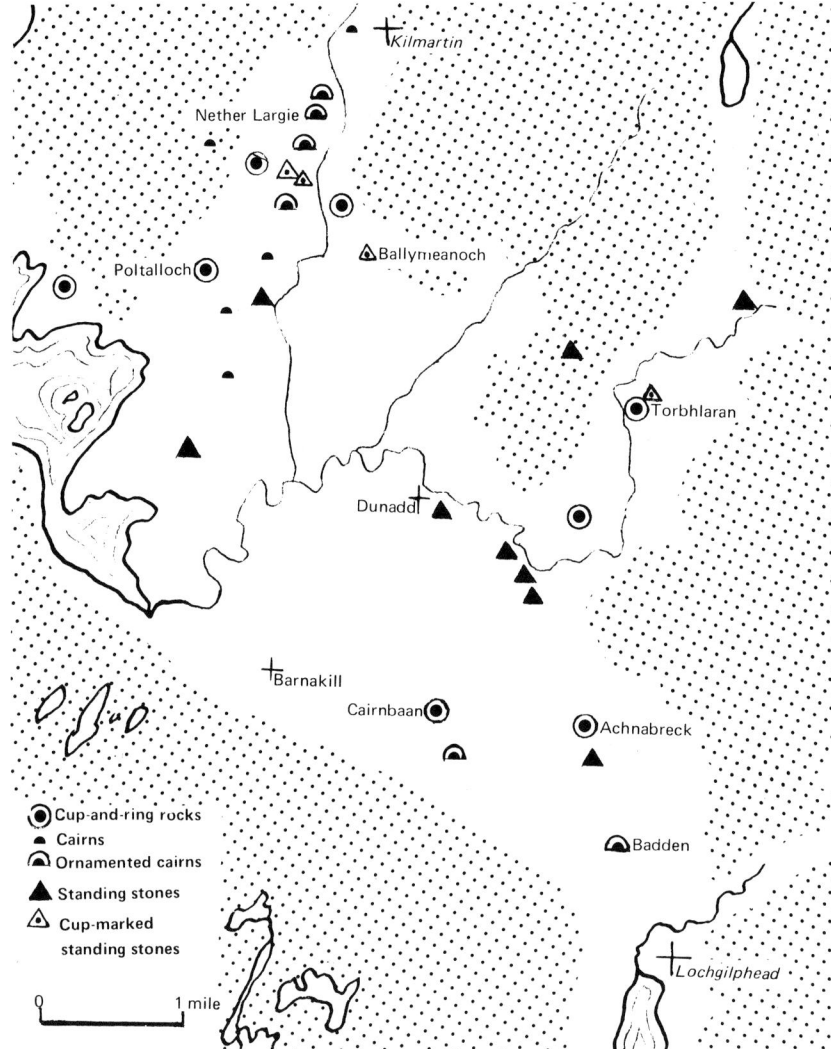

83. Map of the major monuments in the mid-Argyll district.

Kilmartin

Nether Largie

Poltalloch

Ballymeanoch

Torbhlaran

Dunadd

Barnakill

Cairnbaan

Achnabreck

Badden

Lochgilphead

◉ Cup-and-ring rocks
▪ Cairns
◖ Ornamented cairns
▲ Standing stones
△ Cup-marked standing stones

0   1 mile

more surprising when the megalithic tombs of Brittany abound in such representations, notably at La Table des Marchands where a huge hafted axe dominates the art of the chamber. It seems quite clear that the main British traditions had no place for realistic motifs for which we could at once suggest an obvious meaning.

But during the Bronze Age a class of designs appears on the surfaces of a small number of stone cists and other objects that includes not only the accurate outlines of axeheads and daggers, but also footprints and an angular style of abstract ornament. These elements contrast so much with previous carving customs that it is natural to search for some special

84

explanation. The answer can be sought partly in terms of social change within early Bronze Age Britain, in the development from the collective efforts and values which inspired the great stone circles towards a more individualistic society increasingly apparent in the wealth concentrated with a number of single barrow burials. From the broad and widespread range of symbols apparently carved to express common spiritual ideas, we pass to a much more obvious and direct symbol of power, the metal axe, on which the prestige of an aristocracy or chiefdom was founded. It is appropriate that we do not find these images widely scattered on natural rock surfaces for all to see, but mainly associated with a few graves of important individuals.

These assumptions about the development of Bronze Age society are clearly demonstrated at the Kilmartin valley in mid-Argyll, a key route 64 centre for south-west Scotland and also the focus of a major group of cup-and-ring rocks. Travellers could avoid the lengthy journey and dangerous seas around the Kintyre peninsula by an overland shortcut across the fertile plain of Crinan, perhaps continuing northward along the route of the modern road which passes through Kilmartin. Here, stretching in a line from the head of the valley to the shores of Loch Crinan nearly three miles away there grew up a remarkable cemetery of massive round cairns, which seem to reflect the history of an entire dynasty. The sequence begins at Nether Largie South, which was built in the third millennium as a collective chambered tomb and was characteristically re-used for a Beaker burial a number of centuries later. All seven subsequent cairns aligned across the valley cover large stone cists intended for the burial of individuals, and because of slight changes in the contents and structure of the tombs there is good evidence to suppose that the whole cemetery may span as much as 2,000 years of slowly evolving burial customs.

As we have already noted, the cup-and-ring patterns seen at neighbouring sites such as Baluachraig or Poltalloch are not found on the surfaces of the cists. At three of the cairns, the sides and lids of the graves are decorated by carvings in a very different style. The most impressive stone is at Nether Largie North, where the inside surface of the huge covering slab was covered with a haphazard arrangement of cupmarks and axehead shapes. On other stones, notably at Nether Largie mid-cairn and at the Ri Cruin site, other outlines resembling axes can be seen, together with a peculiar pattern originally found at Ri Cruin which has been variously described as a 'ship' (although carved standing upright on its 'stern') or a 'halberd', supposedly with streamers

85

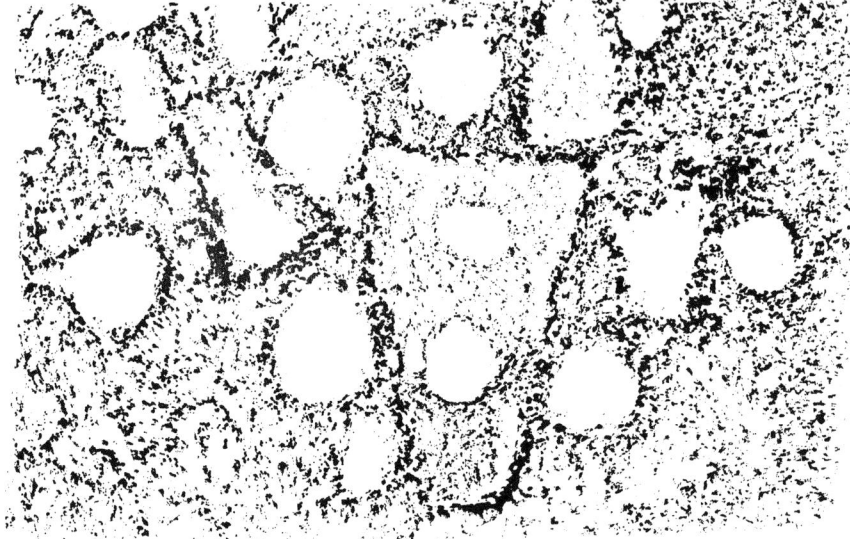

84. Detail of cup and axe outlines on the lower surface of the cist cover from Nether Largie North Cairn, Kilmartin, Argyll. Width of rubbing about 23½ ins (60 cm).

85. The shapes of bronze axes are outlined on a side slab in one of the cists of the Ri Cruin cairn, Kilmartin, Argyll.

flying from its haft. The significant points about this important set of carvings are first that the designs seem to have been matched to the shape of the stone more successfully than in the case of most other

86

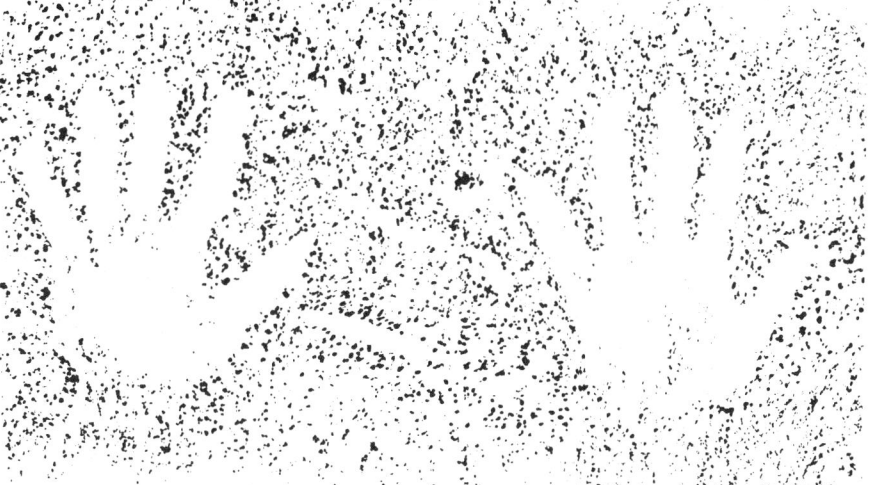

ornamented graves, so they apparently represent an authentic Bronze Age funerary style. Secondly the outlines of the axeheads (and possibly the halberd, if that is what it actually is) correspond to the types of bronze implements that were being traded extensively from Ireland throughout Britain and Europe in the earlier part of the period. They show that Irish influence and the growth of metalworking played some important part in the prosperity of the Kilmartin area.

Yet there is nothing in Ireland remotely resembling the haphazard arrangements of naturalistic designs which are found on the sides and lids of the Kilmartin cists. Instead of looking to the Atlantic seaways for possible sources of this style, we must turn to central Europe and in particular to a group of four large cist and barrow monuments by the River Saale. The crucial point about these German graves is that, like the Kilmartin cists, they owe little or nothing to the traditions of western carving. The closely-set herringbone patterns, either picked, incised or painted on the stones, are divided by vertical and horizontal lines which certainly look as if they are intended to represent decorated textiles hanging from a wall. And there, also 'hanging' on the wall of the dead man's 'house', are the weapons he must have carried in real life, his bow, arrows, daggers and axes. There seems little doubt that the designs on these massive graves (the internal size of the Dölauer Heide cist is 4×1 metres) were meant to reproduce the domestic surroundings of the dead man, perhaps to provide him with such comforts in an after-life. The origins of this idea can be traced convincingly further east to the ornamented 'house-graves' of the Caucasus, and its westernmost influence may well have been on the Breton tombs

65

87. The outlines of a dagger (12 ins or 31 cm long) and axes on stone 53 at Stonehenge.

of Petit Mont and Gavrinis, which show such exceptional all-over decoration.

Could the appearance of realistic carvings on the German cists and in the Kilmartin valley be a coincidence? The depiction of human hands and feet in rock art is largely confined to Scandinavia and northern Europe. So the discovery of a pair of diminutive left hands carved on a boulder by the Crinan Canal, a footprint at Dunadd and a pair of feet 66 at Carnasserie, all lying within two miles of the Kilmartin linear cemetery, should arouse special interest. At the Carnasserie site the feet appear among a cup-and-ring group but this unique combination could well be the result of a secondary addition to the rock surface. A cist cover with footprints and cupmarks from Pool Farm, Somerset, shows 67 that at least one set of these motifs is an authentic Bronze Age carving. The significance of these feet and hand marks is unknown, although in British folklore they are commonly ascribed to the visits of devils and giants to the earth. Their importance to present day studies is the evidence they present of the impact of north European traditions on Britain.

88

The circulation of metal objects—axes, daggers and ornaments—from the great mineral resources of Ireland and south-west Scotland through the prosperous communities of Kilmartin, Wessex, the Saale and further east, encouraged the growth of hierarchies evident at these important route centres in single grave cemeteries of special richness and elaboration. In the trading of daggers it can be shown that the products of the bronze craftsmen of central Europe were particularly in demand by the aristocracy of southern England, whose wealth is most obviously focussed in the barrow burials around Stonehenge. The carvings of daggers and axeheads first noticed there only twenty years ago scattered over a few of the great stones of the temple suggest more than the new spiritual importance of this symbol, more potent and personal than the cup and ring. The Stonehenge carvings reveal something of the widespread economic connections on which the power and   68
achievement represented by the temple were based.

Clearly the suggestion of a link between the Kilmartin and Saale axes is founded on more than a mere coincidence of motifs. A comparison of styles reinforces the arguments, since stones from Argyll sites at Kilchattan, Cairnbaan and Badden are all decorated with geometric ornament quite similar to the German 'textile' carvings. The design of the Badden cist slab, with its repeating lozenges, is perhaps the only one of these stones to suggest an actual woven pattern.

The significance of the lozenge design itself is of considerable interest. In 1808 the celebrated barrow digger, Sir Richard Colt Hoare, uncovered a remarkable golden burial underneath Bush Barrow less than a mile from Stonehenge. His workmen revealed the skeleton of 'a tall and   69
stout man' laid alongside three fine daggers, the haft of one of them inlaid with hundreds of tiny gold pins scattered in every direction by the diggers. Among the exceptional grave goods were a superbly wrought gold scabbard hook and a ceremonial mace with zig-zag bone mounts, obviously a symbol of authority. A small lozenge made from sheet gold decorated a dagger case while on the dead man's breast was a much larger gold lozenge, embellished with a remarkably precise geometrical pattern. The Bush Barrow lozenges are among the most striking examples of craftsmanship ever discovered from a British burial, although ornamented gold plates of similar style are known from other Wessex barrows. Indeed, recent re-examination of these   70
pieces revealed that they were probably all specially produced for funerary purposes, suggested by their lack of wear, and all executed with the use of one engraving tool and presumably at the hands of one

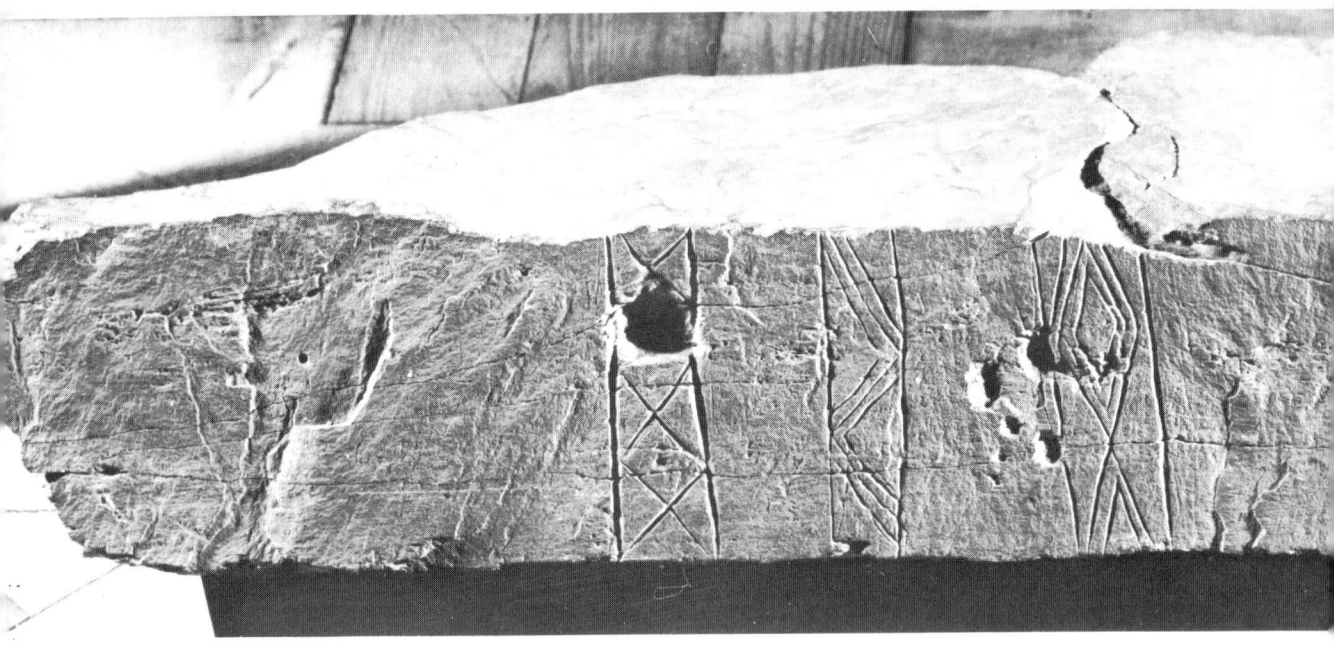

craftsman. So these objects appear to represent the treasures of an influential or ruling group, perhaps a dynasty, closely connected with the centre of power at Stonehenge.

It will be recalled that many centuries previously at Newgrange, the lozenge was carved on more stones than any other motif, and here, close to Stonehenge, the lozenge seems to have been assigned to a man who commanded more respect in death than any other individual of the Bronze Age. In Argyll the lozenge was chosen to decorate two graves at Badden and Cairnbaan. If we recognize this powerful symbol as derived from the passage grave tradition, then its arrangement and embellishment was clearly influenced by a German art style. It may not be too far-fetched to see these lozenges as evidence for some continuity of spiritual values in the face of the economic and social developments that were brought by the Bronze Age. At Kilmartin influences ultimately derived from many places—from Ireland, Wessex and northern Germany—all combined in the decoration of stones which faced the bodies of the privileged dead.

The Cup: Curing and Cursing

There is no clear evidence that the practice of cup-and-ring carving survived the Bronze Age. Ornamented stones are known from quite a number of later sites, such as Iron Age forts and other defensive structures, crannogs or lake settlements, and the underground structures

88. Decorated edge of a sl found lying on two cists ne the Brogar and Stenness sto circles, Orkney. The incis carving is in an angular st which has been compared w single grave art in cent Germany.

90

known as souterrains. In all these cases it is likely that the stones already decorated many centuries before were incorporated, perhaps not always deliberately, into the fabric of the site. The Scottish souterrain builders, however, did display some kind of interest in the cup-and-ring stones at six sites where they are usually found in prominent positions. The souterrains themselves are likely to have served a variety of functions, such as storehouses, dwellings or cattle sheds, corresponding to their different groupings in the western and northern islands and in north-east Scotland. In Angus, where the impressive curved passage-ways up to 200 feet long mainly seem to have housed cattle, two sites at Carlungie I and Ardestie adjoined domestic huts with cup-and-ring stones built into their inside walls. The souterrains are likely to date from the first two or three centuries of the Christian era.

 71

A more direct continuity of tradition, in some places still alive today, is the possible link between basin stones and cupmarking. At a few prehistoric carving sites, notably at Lordenshaws, Northumberland, large circular hollows worked into the rock are visible beside ordinary cup-marks. This may indicate that some of the numerous rock basins which are often the subject of local reverence and folklore in Ireland and elsewhere are artificial and of an early date. The problem of distinguishing this class of marking from a natural erosion hole makes it difficult to establish, as so many antiquaries of the last century thought, that the basins were an active element in the prehistoric traditions of art and religion. Moreover many such hollows were

89/90. (*above left*) A gold lozenge ornament (about 6 ins or 15 cm wide) from Bush Barrow, near Stonehenge, and (*right*) a cist slab from Cairnbaan, Argyll, with a lozenge design.

created for functional purposes as grain mills, which are found on a wide range of ancient sites and were also in common use on Scottish farmhouses up to a century ago. Among the islands of western Argyll, basins near the waterline were formerly used for grinding up bait to catch fish. Mr Ronald Morris collected some interesting stories of the beliefs attached to other non-functional hollows in the same area, starting with the large cup on Seil Island . . .   72

'. . . which has been used for what one might call neo-pagan purposes within living memory. The widow of the late farmer there states that in her youth, one day each spring this basin had by custom to be filled with milk. If it was not so filled, the "wee folk" (fairies) would see that the cows gave no milk that summer. The Kerrera ferryman, to whom I told this, said that on Point of Sleat Farm in Skye when he was a boy there had been exactly the same custom. An Islay resident tells me that the same custom existed there, too, until not long ago and I have received a similar account from Miss Marion Campbell concerning the cup-marked stone near the waterfall beside the old chapel at Cove, Knapdale. . . . In Argyll and its isles the pagan gods are not so long dead.'

91/92. Among the most strangely sited carvings in Britain are these circular and spiral designs at Morwick, Northumberland, which appear on a vertical cliff overhanging the River Coquet, some at a height of 20–25 feet above the present water level. Their odd location suggests that they are not of the same era as the cups and rings, while the style of some is reminiscent of La Tène art of the Iron Age period.

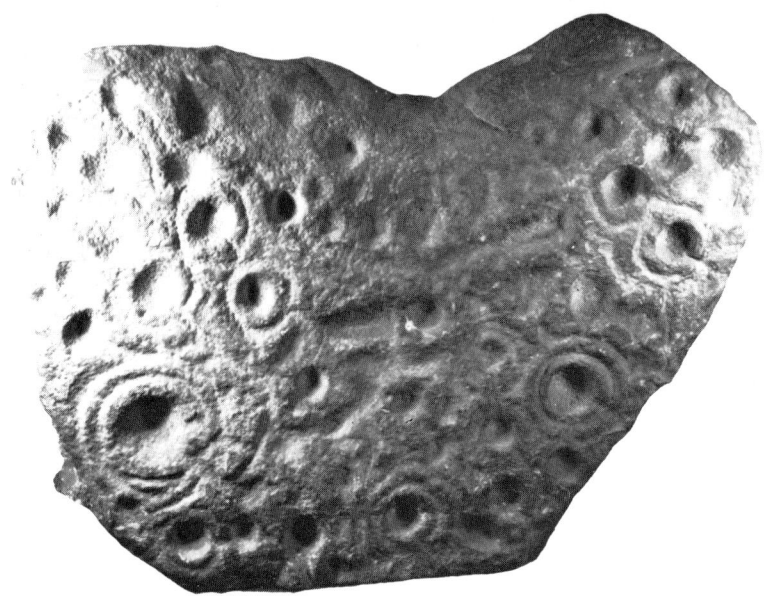

93. A stone decorated on both sides found built into a souterrain at Letham Grange, Angus, and now in Edinburgh's National Museum.

94. The Butter Rolls, near Glengarriff, Co. Cork.

This type of folk-belief lies even closer to the surface of present-day Ireland, where in remote areas large basin stones or bullauns are not hard to find. One of the most incongruously located examples lies in the high street of Dingle, County Kerry, while many others are to be seen in old forts, at the bases of ancient crosses, and in ruined churchyards. The water which gathered in the basins was frequently thought to cure warts or rheumatism, or to correct barrenness in women. Water from a bullaun set in a low mound beside Lough Drumgay, County Fermanagh, cured sore eyes if the rag used for washing was hung on a nearby whitethorn bush. Other basins at church sites have traditionally been used as fonts for baptism, with double hollows customarily explained as the kneeling places of saints.

Much more obviously pagan traditions were associated with 'cursing stones', which were large round pebbles placed in the cavities of the bullaun. The curse against an opponent was uttered while turning the stone clockwise, although it would fall on one's own head if directed against an innocent victim. At the monastic sites of Iona and Innishmurray, cursing stones lay on the pedestals of crosses and on the tops of altars. These were turned three times in honour of the sun, in the direction of its course across the sky, and the end of the world would not come until the supporting stones were worn through. Interestingly enough, among the numerous stones placed on one of the Innishmurray altars was a cup-and-ring slab with a double circle and keyhole carving.

A very remarkable bullaun stone can be seen next to an old graveyard at Temple Feaghna, County Kerry, which features a ring of eight hollows, each with its own rounded pebble, encircling a pestle-shaped stone propped upright in the hole of a grindstone. According to tradition, the pebbles are butter rolls belonging to a woman who attempted to steal Saint Feaghna's butter and was turned into stone. This bullaun was involved in pilgrimages held every Good Friday, Saturday and Easter Sunday, which began with the marking of a cross on a slab of the wall around the graveyard. After walking round the wall three times, visiting the holy well and other devotions, the pilgrim approached the bullaun and turned the stones round once in their holes. Bad luck was sure to befall anyone who removed the butter rolls.

It may well be that the practice of creating these basins is remotely derived from the cup-markings of prehistoric times, although the beliefs and legends associated with them are probably not as ancient. There are a number of instances where these customs. caused offence to the church, for example, in the case of the marble cursing stones

95. Cross-inscribed standing stone at Torran, Argyll.

which were flung into the sea by order of the Iona Synod in the eighteenth century. The practice of carving Christian crosses on ancient monuments of all kinds in order to sanctify them was very widespread. One of the most striking examples is a standing stone at Torran, Argyll, on which a cup-mark is framed by one arm of a cross deeply worked into the stone. A number of crosses appear on cup-marked boulders in Aberdeenshire and beside cup-and-ring patterns in other districts, although it is sometimes difficult to decide whether the cross is a Christian or prehistoric emblem.

By far the strangest case of the apparent Christian accommodation of a pagan symbol is the gravestones from a small group of churchyards on the Dublin–Wicklow border. At Rathmichael there are about half a 76 dozen headstones decorated with concentric circles, while at Dalkey, a few miles north, a slab combines a wheel-headed cross surmounted by concentric circles. The most impressive stone from this group, now in the cellars of the National Museum, was incorporated into the structure of the medieval church at Ballyman, County Dublin. This features a pair of cups surrounded by four rings each, linked by a 'stem' with

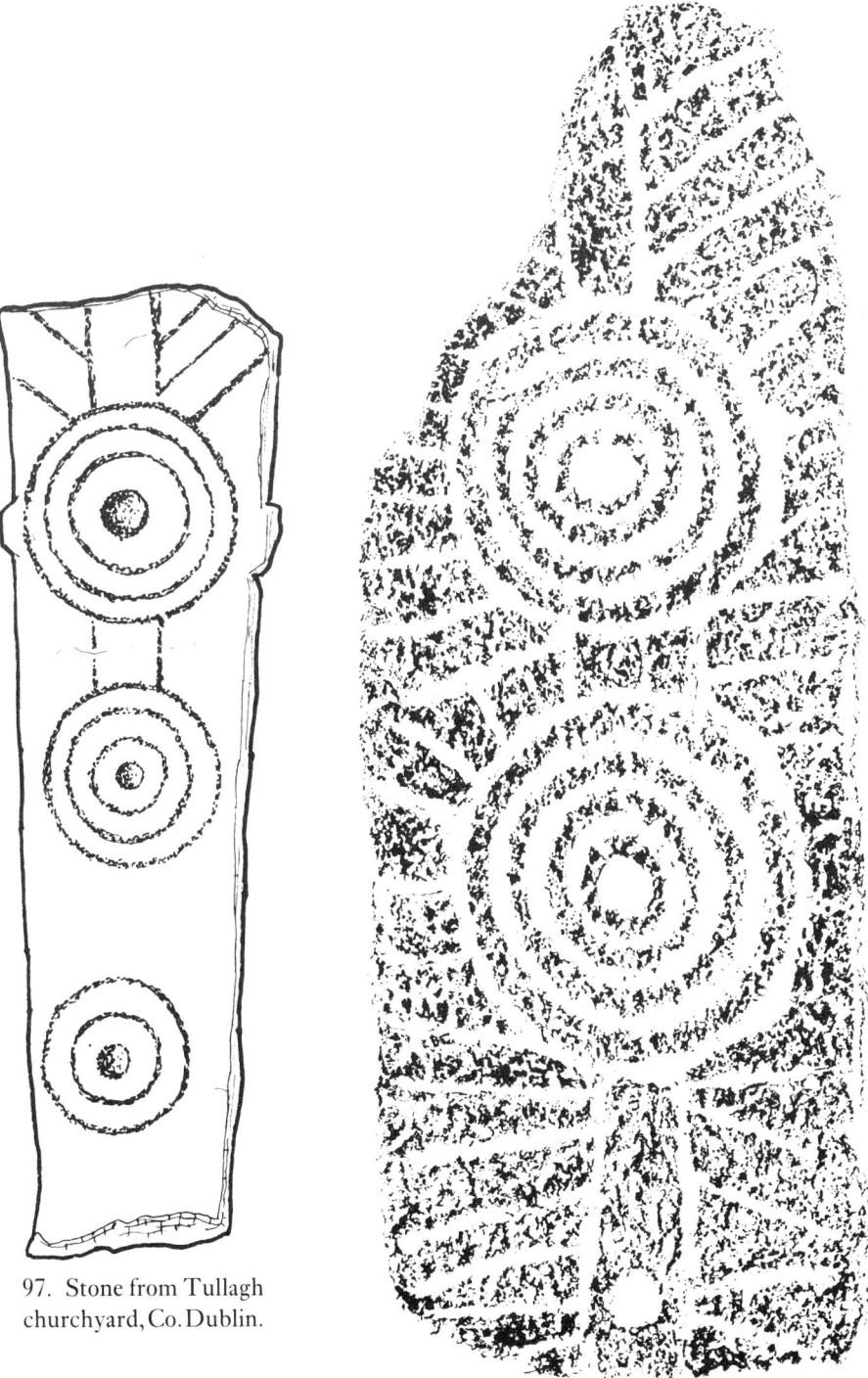

96. The stone from Bally-
man church, Co. Dublin.
Length of stone about 50
ins (130 cm).

97. Stone from Tullagh
churchyard, Co. Dublin.

radiating 'branches' which run off to the sides of the stone. The decorated surface had been partly covered up when it was built into the south window of the church as a lintel, facing downwards. Concentric circles with 'rays' are also known from Killeger and also at Tullagh, where the small stumps projecting from the sides of the slab perhaps indicate a crude attempt to create a sculptured cross.

There is little doubt about the Early Christian origin of these remarkable stones. The monastic enclosures at Rathmichael and Bally-man are probably many centuries older than the churches they surround, while the designs are all found on properly squared-off slabs which are unlikely to be prehistoric. But their real significance is a mystery, especially as they are situated far from any important cup-and-ring group. We can imagine the circles either as independently adopted in Early Christian times, perhaps as a family or kin-group emblem, or else as an extraordinary example of the persistence of one ancient religious convention and its toleration by another.

The Game of Troy

In the course of a chase after a weasel across stony ground at Hollywood, County Wicklow, in 1911, a large granite boulder was overturned revealing a curious pattern which had been carved with immense labour on the flat face. Its earliest investigator, G. H. Orpen, at first thought that the design was a cross with coiling arms 'presenting the general appearance of a pre-Christian spiral'. Closer examination, however, showed that it was different from the circles and spirals of prehistoric times. The Hollywood stone, now preserved in Dublin's National Museum, in fact features a circular labyrinth which draws the eye along a single winding path towards the central cross. To reach the outside, one has to follow the same route back again to the entrance. How this pattern came to Ireland, and the precise origins of the design, form one of the most intriguing unanswered puzzles of European rock art.

What immediate clues were available to suggest a date for the Hollywood stone? It was not possible to trace the fragment of rock which included the rest of the pattern, but carved on a nearby upright stone was a cross with nearly equal arms terminating in cups. The site was in a grassy lane a few hundred yards from the pilgrims' road which led from St Kevin's retreat near Hollywood to the famous monastery he founded in the sixth century at Glendalough. So our first impression of the associations of the Hollywood stone is connected with Early Christian times.

98. The Hollywood stone, Co. Wicklow. Width of rubbing approximately 30 ins (74 cm).

Only one other rock in Britain features the same pattern. Two labyrinths, of an identical form to the Hollywood design except that the pattern is reversed, are to be seen on a vertical outcrop at the secluded Rocky Valley, near Tintagel, Cornwall. The appearance of the Rocky Valley carvings in an area without any other examples of early rock art, and on a vertical surface, should suggest that they are not prehistoric. To confirm this impression, we find that the associations of the area are once again Early Christian. The upper part of the valley was the traditional retreat of St Nectan, while the ruins of the sixth century monastery on the Tintagel promontory are only about a mile to the west. What possible significance could a labyrinth design have for an early Christian?

The origins of the labyrinth stretch far back into ancient times, and have been studied by many writers, of which Matthews' account is still the best. A convenient starting point is the legend of the Minotaur which Theseus slew at the centre of the Cretan labyrinth. When Sir Arthur Evans uncovered the Palace of Knossos at the turn of the century, the intricacy of the corridors and connecting store rooms, together with the plentiful evidence of a bull cult, suggested to him that the legend might have sprung from a basis of historical fact. Certainly by the third century BC the legend was well established because Knossos was issuing coins with labyrinth designs and bull's heads, including the classic circular pattern exactly similar to the Hollywood stone. A graffito scratched on a wall at Pompeii dating to the first century AD shows how this particular pattern had become popularly linked with the legend.

The explanation for the persistence of the circular labyrinth is probably because it was linked with actual rites and ceremonies of the classical epoch. A written account of these performances was left to us by Virgil, who describes funeral games held in honour of Anchises

101. The Game of Troy as depicted on an Etruscan vase of uncertain date.

that included a Troia or display by galloping horsemen. They inter-weaved their courses in

> 'a maze of flight and combat . . . as it is said that in ancient times,
> the labyrinth of rugged Crete had a twisting path of dark walls . . .'

The Game of Troy was so named because the exercise was an ancient and respected custom thought to have originated long ago with the ancestors of Rome itself. The ceremony is mentioned by other authors, and its most vivid illustration, perhaps even earlier than the Knossos coins, is incised on an Etruscan vase, on which a group of mounted figures are followed by the circular labyrinth and the words TRUIA reversed as in a mirror. Pliny makes reference to less impressive labyrinth displays which took place on foot, so that the races and games which were customary at English turf mazes in the medieval period and later seem to have had a classical precedent.

Clearly the 'one-path' type of labyrinth was the most appropriate pattern for processions or displays, and this may well explain its

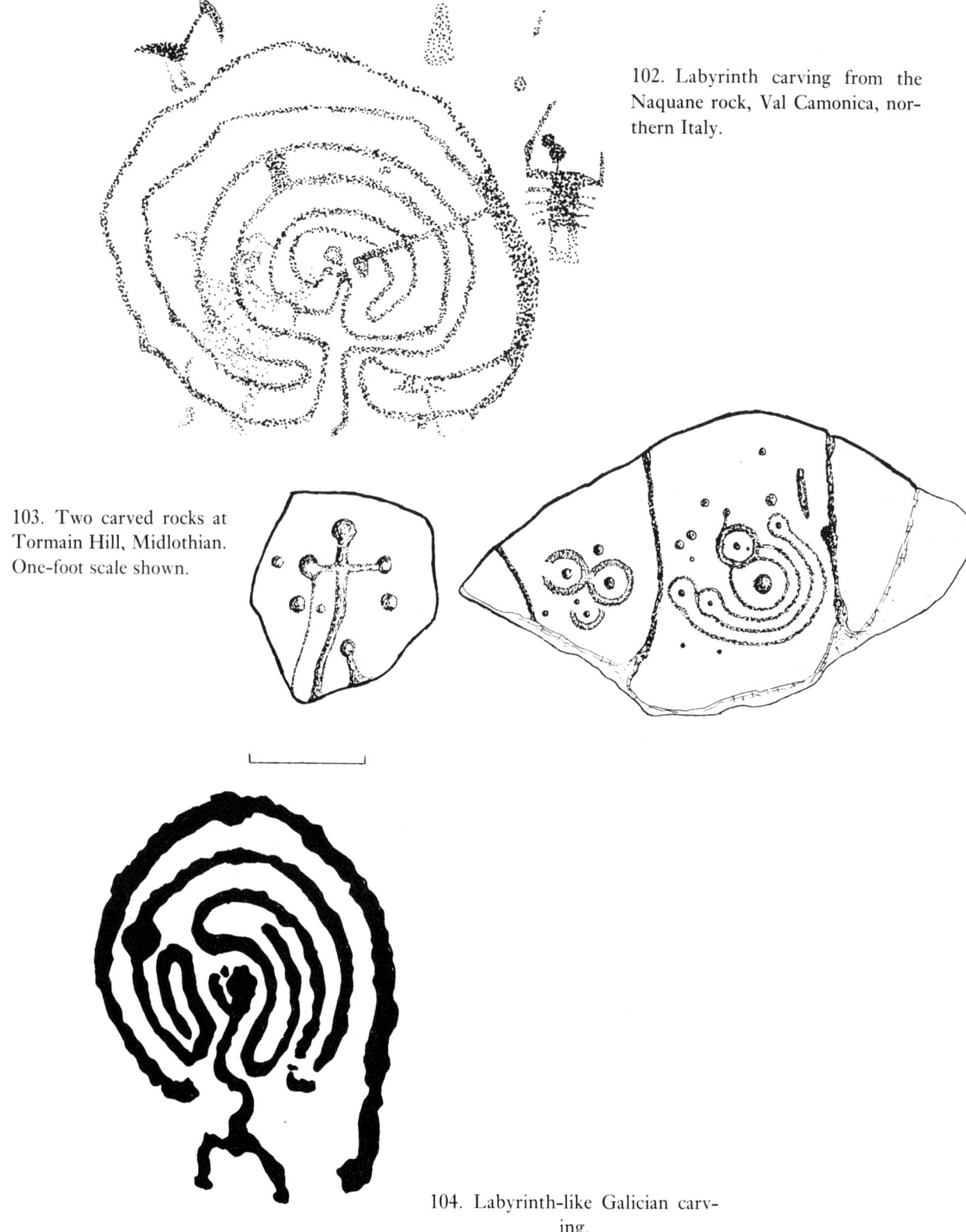

102. Labyrinth carving from the Naquane rock, Val Camonica, northern Italy.

103. Two carved rocks at Tormain Hill, Midlothian. One-foot scale shown.

104. Labyrinth-like Galician carving.

prominence in pre-Christian times. But its appearance was earlier and more widespread than these classical sources would suggest. For example, the labyrinth is one of hundreds of pocked designs on the rock of Naquane, one of the celebrated carving sites of the Val Camonica group near Lake Garda in the Italian Alps. The design here appears to represent some legendary beast, perhaps the Minotaur itself. Then the same pattern can be seen among conventional cup-and-ring carvings at the site of San Jorge de Mogor near Pontevedra and elsewhere in the Galician group of carvings. It would be reasonable, perhaps, to hazard a first millennium BC date for these rock art labyrinths.

78

79

If the pattern was already widespread in Europe in pre-Christian times, could we not also consider the Hollywood stone as prehistoric, perhaps even as a Bronze Age carving linked to the cup-and-ring tradition? Some arguments exist to support this view, since the cross carving with its cup terminals found at the site is not like any conventional type of Early Christian cross. A few complex cup-and-ring designs with portions of the rings closed off, as at Chatton Law, Northumberland, or Tormain Hill, Midlothian, do approach the feeling of a labyrinth design. Moreover as at Hollywood the Tormain Hill pattern appears close to a cross carving which may well be prehistoric. However, it is debateable whether there are any cup-and-ring designs which compare with the systematic layout of the true labyrinth.

80

In any case the spread of the labyrinth design was not solely the result of pre-Christian myth and ceremony. During the Empire the ancient symbol dignified the mosaic pavements of wealthy Romans and, according to an early Florentine manuscript, adorned the robes of the Emperor himself. It is hardly surprising that the labyrinth became a part of Christian iconography and decorated the walls and floors of early churches. The third century floor of the Orleansville basilica was centred around an acrostic of SANCTA ECCLESIA, representing the spiritual peace which could only be reached at the end of the twisting path of life. This type of allegorical meaning is the subject of an inscription at the Church of San Savino at Piacenza, which taught that the labyrinth carving there stood for life, broad at the entrance and narrow at its exit; a man once ensnared by joys and vices could keep to his path only with difficulty. Labyrinth designs were widely used as church pavements during the thirteenth century, notably at cathedrals such as Chartres, Amiens, Bayeux and Rheims. The Christian symbolism of these designs was made explicit by the division of the pattern into quadrants around a cross shape. The fact that most English turf-mazes are of this pattern is a strong reason for supposing that the practice of cutting them began during medieval times in imitation of the church labyrinths. In Shakespeare's day the custom of races and processions was popular, for in *A Midsummer Night's Dream* Titania tells us that

> 'The quaint mazes in the wanton green
> For lack of tread are indistinguishable'

From eighteenth century sources we know that certain mazes such as those at Pimperne, Somerton and Burgh were nick-named the Walls of Troy, and so there seems to have been a popular consciousness of the classical origins of this sport.

In areas less exposed to ecclesiastical contacts with France, the Hollywood type of labyrinth seems to have prevailed. Pebble labyrinths are found in a number of Baltic countries, while such a design apparently existed on a Danish cross of the Viking Age. In a book on the antiquities of Wales printed in 1815, Roberts describes the 'city of Troy' which was sometimes cut by shepherd boys in turf, again corresponding to the Hollywood pattern. The difficulty is to know whether both varieties of labyrinth were brought to northern Europe by the Church in medieval times, or whether the Hollywood design represents an older tradition. If so, then there is not much to help us decide if it came to Cornwall, Wicklow and perhaps Wales through some Early Christian monastic source, or else by even earlier contact with pre-Christian myth which certainly reached as far as western Portugal. Perhaps the labyrinth is matched only by the cup and ring for ambiguity of period and meaning, spanning so many possible eras and revealing our ignorance of its real place among Europe's earliest symbols in stone.

Notes on the Text

1. For the folklore of the Boyne tombs, see Conwell 1864–6 and C. O'Kelly 1971. For associations in early historical times, Ó Corráin 1972 and Byrne 1968.

2. From a letter to Dr Tancred Robinson dated Dec 15 1699, in Tr Royal Soc, Abr Ser V 1703–12 p. 694. Early antiquarian accounts of Newgrange are discussed in Herity 1967, C. O'Kelly 1971 p. 72–4 and also in Ó Ríordáin and Daniel 1964 p. 30–46.

3. See C. O'Kelly 1971 for authoritative account of excavations.

4. Dowth excavations summarized in Wilde 1849, Coffey 1912 p. 44–60 and Ó Ríordáin and Daniel 1964 p. 65–72.

5. Since excavations of Knowth are still in progress, no full publication is available. Useful summaries of kerb art and satellites in Eogan 1968 and 1974, and of main passage graves in Eogan 1963, 1967, 1969 and in *CA* 22 1970 p. 292–296.

6. See Conwell 1864–6 and Piggott 1954 p. 202–208.

7. Excavations reported in Hartnett 1957.

8. A discussion of the roof-box and its function can be found in C. O'Kelly 1971 p. 92–95 and p. 114, and in Patrick 1974.

9. For a general account of Tara, see Ó Ríordáin 1964.

10. The frequency of Newgrange motifs is discussed in M. J. O'Kelly 1970 and in C. O'Kelly 1973.

11. The motifs are analysed in Miss Shee's 1968 Corpus and her 1972 *Bolletino* article. See also C. O'Kelly 1973.

12. Refer to C. O'Kelly 1971, p. 104–110.

13. Excavations reported by Hemp 1930 but see crucial reinterpretation by C. O'Kelly 1969.

14. Described in Powell and Daniel 1956.

15. M. J. O'Kelly 1970.

16. See Simpson and Thawley 1972 for a thorough discussion of single grave art, but note criticisms of Shee 1972a.

17. Wainwright and Longworth 1971 p. 70–1.

18. Edwardson 1965.

19. Greenwell 1890, for full illustrations see plates I and II.

20. Simpson and Thawley 1972 p. 92.

21. The best general introduction to megalithic tombs is still Daniel 1958. This should be read side-by-side with Renfrew 1967 and Daniel 1967a.

22. Savory 1968 provides details of Iberian sites.

23. Renfrew 1967.

24. See Giot 1971 p. 208–217 and Shee 1972 p. 220–2.

25. Discussed in Eogan 1968 p. 352–4.

26. The Iberian connections are summarized in O Riordáin and Daniel 1964 p. 126–135. For ornamented plaques see Leisners 1943/1956. For tomb art Savory 1968 p. 110–113 and for particularly fine illustrations of rock art Anati 1968.

27. See the corpus of Breton tomb art, Péquart and Le Rouzic 1927.

28. Eogan 1967. But see the authoritative summary of Boyne art connections in C. O'Kelly 1973 p. 379–380.

29. The article by Rev James Graves 1876–8 contains a reprint of the original paper by Rev Charles Graves. Greenwell's theories are quoted in Collingwood Bruce 1869.

30. As mentioned in Piggott 1958 p. 61 and 1962 p. 92.

31. The Strath Tay carvings are discussed by Stewart 1958–9 p. 76–80. For a summary of the metal-working theory as applied to southern Scotland, see Morris 1967–8 p. 51–52.

32. See Le Rouzic 1930 and Burl 1972.

33. Graves 1876–8 p. 291.

34. Thom 1968 and 1969. For the wider aspects of Professor Thom's work, see *Megalithic Sites in Britain* and *Megalithic Lunar Observatories*. The subject of the megalithic yard has been discussed in private communications to the author by B. R. Hallam, Dr J. Hudson, Professor D. G. Kendall, J. Patrick and others.

35. See note 31. All Mr Morris's papers are invaluable for obtaining a clear picture of the southern Scottish carvings.

36. Raistrick 1934–6 and Cowling 1936–8 and 1946.

37. The Northumbrian groups are illustrated by Tate 1865 and their distribution shown in Dodds ed., 1935 and 1940. The Lordenshaws site is described in detail in Newbigin 1932.

38. Allen 1896.

39. These details are published by courtesy of Miss M. Campbell, Miss K. Lindsay-MacDougall and the Natural History and Antiquarian Society of Mid Argyll.

40. The Dalladies excavations are described in Piggott 1973.

41. Piggott and Powell 1948–9.

42. For the Clava theories, see Henshall 1963 and 1972, and also Burl 1972.

43. The astronomy of Clava-type monuments has been most recently discussed by Burl 1972 p. 43–46.

44. Monzie excavation reported in Young and Mitchell 1938–9.

45. Balnuaran excavation in Piggott 1954–6.

46. Culcharron cairn reported by Peltenburg 1972.

47. Croft Moraig by Piggott and Simpson 1971.

48. For art associated with round barrows see Ashbee 1958 and 1960 p. 66–68.

49. The Temple Wood spiral is published by courtesy of Dr Aubrey Burl.

50. See note 43.

51. The Caherlehillan spiral published by Macalister in 1939 has been shown to be concentric circles by Miss F. Finlay. Her 1973 corpus is the key reference for the Irish cup-and-ring carvings.

52. This is the subject of a paper by M. J. O'Kelly and E. A. Shee 1971.

53. The area is thoroughly surveyed by Morris and Bailey 1964–66. The author's examination of the Cauldside Burn carving, verified by Mr Morris, has established it as a spiral.

54. From Macalister 1928 p. 94–96. For the recent analysis of the Clonfinlough stone, see Jackson 1967, and for the Abbé Breuil's remarks, see his 1934 *Address*, p. 317.

55. The Galician rock art and its connections have been described in Savory 1968 p. 209–212 and illustrated in the *Corpus* of Sobrino–Buhigas 1935 and in Anati 1968.

56. See references in Simpson and Thawley 1972 p. 89.

57. *Valcamonica Symposium* p. 135–142.

58. Quoted in Rivett–Carnac 1879 p. 15.

59. See Levy 1948 p. 50–52.

60. As quoted by Mallery 1888–9 p. 200.

61. For an excellent summary of Scandinavian rock art and associated beliefs, see Gelling and Davidson 1969.

62. There is a fine display of these axes in Edinburgh's National Museum of Antiquities.

63. See Giot 1960 p. 109–114.

64. A summary account of the Kilmartin monuments can be found in Scott 1966 p. 35–41. For a more detailed discussion, with references, see Campbell, Scott and Piggott 1960–1. An inventory of the monuments and cup-and-ring rocks in the area appears in Campbell and Sandeman 1961–2.

65. The best English account of these monuments is Powell 1960.

66. For a note on the hands at Barnakill, see Dickie 1963–4. For other naturalistic carvings, see inventory of Campbell and Sandeman 1961–2.

67. See Grinsell 1957.

68. Some of these social questions are usefully discussed in Renfrew 1973.

69. The 'excavation' is described in Ashbee 1960 p. 76–78.

70. See Coles and Taylor 1971.

71. See the discussion of these stones in Wainwright 1963.

72. Morris 1967–8 p. 55.

73. See the comprehensive article on bullauns in Crozier and Rea 1940.

74. See Wakeman 1893.

75. Crozier and Rea 1940 p. 108–109.

76. The gravestones are described and illustrated in Drew 1868–9, Purefoy Colles 1870 and Graves 1876–8.

77. For the debate on the Hollywood stone, see Orpen 1923 and Bremer 1926–7.

78. There is a good photograph of the Naquane labyrinth in *Valcamonica Symposium* p. 229.

79. See the *Corpus* of Sobrino–Buhigas 1935 figs. 166–170.

80. The Chatton Law stone is illustrated by Tate 1865 plate X fig. 1, and Tormain Hill by Allen 1881–2 p. 82–85.

Sources of Illustrations

The author is grateful to the following for permission to reproduce photographs:

Trustees of the British Museum, 28, 29, 82, 89; Commissioners for Pu lic Works in Irel1nd, 13, 14, 21, 36; Educational Expeditions International, 65, 85, 95; Green Studio Ltd, 12; National Museum of Antiqutities of Scotl1nd, 30, 61, 62, 90, 93; R. W. B. Morris, 43; M. J. O'Kelly, 8; J. Patrick, 7, 11, 22; Pictorial Colour Slides, 87; A. Thom, 43.

The text figures are based on the following originals:

9, after C. O'Kelly 1971; 26, after Fergusson 1872; 31, after Leisners 1956 Taf 7; 35, after P´quart and Le Rouzic 1927; 50, after Raistrick 1933 and Cowling 1946; 51, after Dodds 1935 and 1939; 81, after Sobrino-Buhigas 1935; 97, after Purefoy Colles 1870–1; 100, 101, after Matthews 1922; 102, after Valcamonica Symposium 1970; 103, after Allen 1881–2; 104, after Anati 1968.

The two main distribution maps, 27 1nd 76, were based on MacWhite 1946, Simpson 1nd Thawley 1972 1nd other sources, but in view of the comments in Shee 1972a, not much reliance should be placed on the positions of cists shown. The information for 67 was supplied by Dr Aubrey Burl.

List of Useful Works

Passage Graves and their Background

Anati, E. G., 1968. *Arte rupestre nelle Regioni occidentali della Penisola Iberica*, Edizioni del Centro, Capo di Ponte.

Daniel, G. E., 1950. *The Prehistoric Chamber Tombs of England and Wales*, Cambridge U. P.
       1958. *The Megalith Builders of Western Europe*, Pelican.
       1960. *The Prehistoric Chamber Tombs of France*, Thames and Hudson.
       1967. *The Origins and Growth of Archaeology*, Pelican.
       1967a. *Northmen and Southmen* in *Ant* XLI p. 313–17.

Giot, P. R., 1960. *Brittany*, Thames and Hudson.
       1971. *The impact of radiocarbon dating . . .* in *PPS* XXXVII Part II p. 208–217.

Henshall, A. S., 1963. *The Chamber Tombs of Scotland Vol I*, Edinburgh U. P.
       1972. *Vol II*.

Herity, M., 1970. *The Early Prehistoric Period around the Irish Sea*, from *The Irish Sea Province in Archaeology and History*, Cambrian Archaeological Association.

Leisner, G. and V., 1943 and 1956. *Die Megalithgraber der Iberischen Halbinsel*, Berlin.

Péquart, M. and St J., and Le Rouzic, Z., 1927. *Corpus des Signes Gravés des Monuments Megalithiques du Morbihan*.

Piggott, S., 1965. *Ancient Europe*, Edinburgh U. P.

Place, R., 1968. *Introduction to Archaeology*, Newnes.

Renfrew, C., 1967. *Colonialism and Megalithismus*, in *Ant* XLI p. 276–288.
       1973. *Before Civilization*, Jonathan Cape.

Roe, D., 1971. *Prehistory*, Paladin.

Savory, H. N., 1968. *Spain and Portugal*, Thames and Hudson.

Shee, E. A., 1972. *Recent Work on Irish Passage Graves Art*, in *Bollettino del Centro Camuno di Studi Preistorici* Vol VIII p. 220–222 for Brittany dates.

Byrne, F. J., 1968. *Historical Note on Cnogba (Knowth)* in *PRIA* Vol 66c p. 383–400.

CA 1970. *Knowth, New Grange* in No 22 p. 292–300.

Coffey, G., 1896. *Origins of Prehistoric Ornament in Ireland*, in *JRSAI* VIII and IX p. 34–69.
1912. *New Grange*, Hodges and Figgis, Dublin.

Conwell, E. A., 1864–6. *Examination of the Ancient Sepulchral Cairns on the Loughcrew Hills, County of Meath*, in *PRIA* IX p. 42–50 and 355–379.
1873. *Discovery of the Tomb of Ollamh Fodhla*, Dublin.

Edwardson, A. R., 1965. *A spirally decorated object from Garboldisham*, in *Ant* XXXIX p. 145.

Eogan, G., 1963. *A new passage-grave in Co. Meath*, in *Ant* XXXVII p. 226–8.
1963a. *A neolithic habitation-site and megalithic tomb in Townleyhall townland, Co. Louth*, in *JRSAI* Vol 93 p. 37–81.
1967. *The Knowth (Co. Meath) excavations*, in *Ant* XLI p. 302–4.
1968. *Excavations at Knowth, Co. Meath*, in *PRIA* Vol 66c p. 299–400.
1968a. *Irish tomb 4500 years ago*, in *Illustrated London News* May 4 p. 25–27.
1969. *Excavations at Knowth, Co. Meath, 1968*, in *Ant* XLIII p. 8–14.
1974. *Report on the Excavation of Some Passage Graves . . .*, in *PRIA* Vol 74c.

Forde-Johnson, J. L., 1957. *Megalithic art in the North-West of Britain; the Calderstones, Liverpool*, in *PPS* XXIII p. 20–39.

Frazer, W., 1893. *Notes on Incised Sculpturings of Stones in the cairns of Sliabh-na-Calliaghe, near Loughcrew, Co. Meath*, in *PSAS* XXVII p. 294–340.

Greenwell, W., 1890. *Recent Researches in Barrows . . .*, in *Archaeol* LII p. 14–15.

Hartnett, P. J., 1957. *Excavation of a Passage Grave at Fourknocks, County Meath*, in *PRIA* Vol 58c p. 197–277.

Hemp, W. J., 1930. *The chambered cairn of Bryn-Celli-ddu*, in *Archaeol* LXXX p. 179–214.

Herity, M., 1967. *From Lhuyd to Coffey*, in *Studia Hibernica* Vol 7 p. 127–145.

Leask, H. G., 1933. *Inscribed stones recently discovered at Dowth tumulus, Co. Meath*, in *PRIA* Vol 41c p. 162–167.

Lynch, F., *Barclodiad-y-Gawres, comparative notes on the decorated stones*, in *Arch Cambr* CXVI p. 1–22.

Macalister, R. A. S., 1943. *A preliminary report on the excavation of Knowth*, in *PRIA* Vol 49c p. 131–166.

Ó Corráin, D., 1972. *Ireland before the Normans*, Gill and Macmillan, see p. 68.

O'Kelly, C., 1969. *Bryn-celli-ddu, Anglesey, A reinterpretation*, in *Arch Cambr* CXVIII p. 17–48.
1971. *Guide to Newgrange*, John English, Wexford.
1973. *Passage-grave art in the Boyne Valley, Ireland*, in *PPS* XXXIX p. 354–382.

O'Kelly, M. J., 1964. *Newgrange, Co. Meath*, in *Ant* XXXVIII p. 288–290.
1967. *Two examples of megalithic art from the Newgrange area*, in *JRSAI* Vol 97 p. 45–46.
1968. *Excavations at Newgrange, Co. Meath*, in *Ant* XLII p. 40–42.
1969. *Radiocarbon dates for the Newgrange passage-grave, Co. Meath*, in *Ant* XLIII p. 140.
1970. *Newgrange passage-grave, Ireland, the mural art*, *Actes du VII Congres Int. des Sc. Prehist. et Protoh.*, Prague, p. 534–536.

Ó Nualláin, S., 1968. *A ruined megalithic cemetery in Co. Donegal . . .* , in *JRSAI* XCVIII p. 1–29.

Ó Riordáin, S. P., 1968. *Tara: the Monuments on the Hill*, Dundalgan Press, Dundalk.

Ó Riordáin, S. P. and Daniel, G. E., 1964. *New Grange*, Thames and Hudson.

Patrick, J., 1974. *Midwinter sunrise at Newgrange*, in *Nature* Vol 249 p. 517–519.

Piggott, S., 1954. *The Neolithic Cultures of the British Isles*, Chapter VII.

Powell, T. G. E., 1938. *The passage graves of Ireland*, in *PPS* IV p. 239–248, and Daniel, G. E., 1956. *Barclodiad y Gawres*. Liverpool U. P.

Rynne, E., 1963. *The decorated stones at Seefin*, in *JRSAI* XCIII p. 85–86.

Shee, E. A., 1968. Unpublished corpus of non-Boyne valley art.
    1972. *Recent Work on Irish Passage Grave Art*, in *Bollettino del Centro Camuno di Studi Preistorici* Vol VIII p. 199–224.
    1972a. *Three Decorated Stones from Loughcrew*, Co. Meath, in *JRSAI* Vol 102 p. 224–233.
    (in the press). *The techniques of Irish passage grave art*, occasional publication of the Jutland Arch. Soc., Denmark.

Simpson, D. D. A., and Thawley, J. E., 1972. *Single Grave Art in Britain*, in *SAF* No 4, see p. 84–92.

Wainwright, G. J., and Longworth, I. H., 1971. *Durrington Walls: Excavations* 1966–68, Society of Antiquaries, London, see p. 70–71.

Wakeman, W. F., 1891. *On several sepulchral scribings and rock markings*, in *JRSAI* XV p. 538–560.

Wilde, W. R., 1849. *The Beauties of the Boyne and its Tributary the Blackwater*, 3rd edtn 1949, Dublin.

British Rock Art: Background Material

Ashbee, P., 1958. *The Excavation of Tregulland Burrow*, in *Ant Jnl* XXXVIII p. 174.
    1960. *The Bronze Age Round Barrow in Britain*, Phoenix, London.

Atkinson, R. J. C., 1956. *Stonehenge*, Hamish Hamilton, London, p. 30–34.

Breuil, H., 1934. *Presidential Address*, *PPS* VIII p. 289–322.

Browne, G. F., 1921. *On Some Antiquities in the Neighbourhood of Dunecht House*, Aberdeenshire, Cambridge U. P.

Coles, J. M., and Taylor, J., 1971. *The Wessex culture: a minimal view*, in *Ant* XLV p. 6–14.

Collingwood, Bruce, J., 1869. *Incised markings on stone . . .*, London.

Daniel, G. E., 1950. *The Prehistoric Chamber Tombs of England and Wales*, Cambridge U. P., p. 115–120.

Grinsell, L. V., 1957. *A decorated cist slab from Mendip*, in *PPS* XXIII p. 231–2.

MacWhite, E., 1946. *A new view on the Irish Bronze Age rock scribings*, in *JRSAI* Vol 76 p. 59–80.

Mann, L. M., 1915. *Archaic Sculpturings*, Hodge.

Morris, R. W. B., 1969. *The Cup-and-Ring Marks and Similar Early Sculptures of Scotland*, in *Tr Anc Mons Soc* XVI, see p. 48–51.

Paley Baildon, W., 1909. *The Classification of 'Cup and Ring' Carvings*, in *Archaeol* LXI p. 361.

Renfrew, C., 1973. *Wessex as a social question*, in *Ant* XLVII p. 221–225.

Simpson, J. Y., 1865. *On Ancient Sculpturings of cups and concentric rings . . .*, *PSAS* VI, Appendix, p. 1–140.

Simpson, D. D. A., and Thawley, J. E., *Single Grave Art in Britain*, in *SAF* No 4 p. 81–104.

Tate, G., 1865. *The Ancient British Sculptured Rocks of Northumberland . . .*, Alnwick, also in *BNC* V p. 137–178.

Thom, A., 1966. *Megalithic astronomy: indications in standing stones*, in *Vistas in Astronomy* Vol 7, see p. 54–55.

1968. *The metrology and geometry of cup and ring marks*, in *Systematics* Vol 6 p. 173–189.

1969. *The geometry of cup-and-ring marks*, in *Tr Anc Mons Soc* Vol 16 p. 77–87.

See also *Megalithic Sites in Britain*, Oxford U. P. 1967, and *Megalithic Lunar Observatories*, Oxford U. P. 1971.

Wise, T. A., 1884. *History of Paganism in Caledonia*, see p. 49–69.

Rock Art of Northern England

Allen, R., 1896. *'Cup and Ring' Sculptures on Ilkley Moor*, in *Reliquary* Vol II.

Collingwood Bruce, J., 1869. *Incised markings on stone . . .* , London.

Cowling, E. T., 1936–8. *Cup and ring markings to the north of Otley*, in *YAJ* XXXIII p. 291–297.
   1946. *Rombalds Way. A Prehistory of Mid-Wharfedale*.

Dodds, M. H., ed., 1899, *A History of Northumberland*, Vol V p. 334. (Morwick carvings).
   1935. *Vol XIV* p. 46–67. (List of sites in Doddington region and discussion).
   1940. *Vol XV* p. 42–62. (Coquetdale sites and discussion). All volumes Reid & Co, Newcastle.

Gunn, W., 1885–6. *Undescribed Sculptured Rocks*, in *BNC* XI p. 401–2. (Fowberry Park).

Heywood, N., 1888. *Cup and Ring Stones near Ilkley*, in *Tr Lancs & Chesh Ant Soc* VI p. 127–8.

Hogg, A. H. A., & N., 1956. *Doddington and Horton Moors*, in *AA* XXXIV 4th Series p. 142–149.

Newbigin, E. R., 1932. *Incised Rocks at Lordenshaws*, in *AA* IX 4th Series p. 50–67.

Raistrick, A., 1934–6. *'Cup and Ring' Marked Rocks of West Yorkshire*, in *YAJ* XXXII p. 33–42.

Tate, G., 1865. *The Ancient British Sculptured Rocks of Northumberland . . .* , Alnwick, also in *BNC* V p. 137–178.

Rock Art of Scotland

Allen, R., 1881–2. *Notes on some undescribed stones with cup-markings in Scotland*, in *PSAS* XVI p. 79–143.

Burl, A., 1972. *Stone Circles and Ring-Cairns*, in *SAF* No 4 p. 31–47.

Campbell, M., and Sandeman, M., 1961–2. *Mid Argyll, An Archaeological Survey*, in *PSAS* XCV p. 1–126, and Scott, J. G., and Piggott, S., 1960–1. *The Badden Cist Slab*, in *PSAS* XCIV p. 46–61.

Dickie, J. M., 1963–4. *Carved hands on a boulder at Barnakill, Argyll*, in *PSAS* XCVII p. 249.

Edwards, A. J. H., 1935. *Rock Sculpturings on Traprain Law, E. Lothian*, in *PSAS* LXIX p. 122–137.

Henshall, A. S., 1963. *The Chambered Tombs of Scotland, Vol I*, Edinburgh U. P., see p. 12–39.
        1972, *Vol II*, see p. 270–276.

Morris, R. W. B., and Bailey, D. C., 1964–6. *The Cup-and-Ring Marks and Similar Sculptures of South-Western Scotland: A Survey*, in *PSAS* XCVII p. 150–172.

Morris, R. W. B., 1966–7. *The Cup-and-Ring Marks and Similar Sculptures of South-West Scotland*, in *Tr Anc Mons Soc* Vol 14 p. 77–117.
        1967–8. *The Cup-and-Ring Marks and Similar Sculptures of Scotland: a Survey of the Southern Counties, Part II*, in *PSAS* XCIX p. 47–58.
        1969. *The Cup and Ring Marks and Similar Early Sculptures of Scotland, Part 2*, in *Tr Anc Mons Soc* Vol 16 p. 37–67.

Peltenburg, E. J., 1972. *Culcharron Cairn, Benderloch, Argyll*, in *SAF* No 4 p. 50–51.

Piggott, S., and Powell, T. G. E., 1948–9. *The Excavation of three Neolithic Chamber Tombs in Galloway*, in *PSAS* LXXXIII, see p. 118 and plate XXVI.

Piggott, S., 1954–6. *Excavations in Passage-Graves and Ring-Cairns of the Clava Group*, 1952–3, in *PSAS* LXXXVIII p. 171–207.
        1958. *Scotland Before History*, Nelson.
        1962. *The Prehistoric Peoples of Scotland*, Routledge & Kegan Paul.
        and Simpson, D. D. A., 1971. *Excavation of a Stone Circle at Croft Moraig, Perthshire, Scotland*, in *PPS* XXXVII p. 1–15.
        1973. *The Dalladies long barrow: NE Scotland*, in *Ant* XLVII p. 32–36.

Ritchie, J. N. G., and A., 1972. *Edinburgh and South-East Scotland*, Heinemann Educational Books.

Scott, J. G., 1966. *South-West Scotland*, Heinemann Educational Books.

Stewart, M. E. C., 1958–9. *Strath Tay in the Second Millennium BC*, in *PSAS* XCIV, see p. 76–80.

Wainwright, F. T., 1963. *The Souterrains of Southern Pictland*, Routledge and Kegan Paul.

Young, A., and Mitchell, M. C., 1938–9. *Report on Excavation at Monzie*, in *PSAS* LXXIII p. 62–70.

Rock Art of Ireland

Anati, E. G., 1963. *New Petroglyphs at Derrynablaha, County Kerry, Ireland*, in *JCHAS* LXVIII p. 1–15.

Bremer, W., 1926–7. *Note on the Hollywood Stone*, in *JRSAI* XLVI p. 51–54.

Crozier, I. R., and Rea, L. C., 1940. *Bullauns and other Basin-Stones*, in *UJA* III p. 104–114.

Drew, T., 1868–9. *Proceedings, JKAS* I 3rd series p. 439–442.

Finlay, F., 1973. Unpublished corpus of south-west Irish rock scribings.

Graves, J., 1876–8. *On Cup and Circle Sculptures as Occurring in Ireland*, in *JKAS* IV 4th Series p. 283–296.

Jackson, J. S., 1967. *The Clonfinlough Stone: a Geological Assessment*, in *North Munster Studies*, ed. E. T. Rynne, Thomond Archaeological Society, Limerick.

Macalister, R. A. S., 1928. *The Archaeology of Ireland*, Methuen.
          1939. *A Monument with Bronze-Age Scribings in Co. Kerry*, in *PRIA* Vol 45c p. 21–23.

MacWhite, E., 1946. *A new view on the Irish Bronze Age rock scribings*, in *JRSAI* Vol 76 p. 59–80.

O'Kelly, M. J., 1958. *A new group of Rock-Scribings in Co. Kerry*, in *JCHAS* LXIII p. 1–4, and Shee, E. A., 1971. *The Derrynablaha 'Shield' Again*, in *JCHAS* LXXVI p. 72–76.

Orpen, G. H., 1923. *The Hollywood Stone and the Labyrinth of Knossos*, in *JRSAI* XLIII p. 177–189.

Purefoy Colles, J. A., 1870–1. *Proceedings, JKAS* I 4th Series p. 208–211.

Shee, E. A., 1968. *Some examples of Rock-art from County Cork*, in *JCHAS* LXXIII p. 144–151.

Wakeman, W. F., 1893. *A Survey of the Antiquarian Remains on the Island of Inismurray*, Williams & Norgate.

Rock Art of Other Countries

Anati, E. G., 1968. *Arte rupestre nelle Regioni occidentali della Penisola Iberica*, Edizioni del Centro, Capo di Ponte.

Fett, E. O. P., 1941. *Sydvestnorske Helleristninger*, Stavanger.

Gelling, P., and Davidson, H. E., 1972. *The Chariot of the Sun*, Aldine paperback.

Giot, P. R., 1960. *Brittany*, Thames & Hudson.

Glob, P. V., 1969. *Helleristninger i Danmark*, Jutland Arch Soc Pub Vol VII, with English summary.

Knight, W. F. J., 1932. *Maze Symbolism and the Troy Game*, in *Ant* VI p. 445–458.

Kuhn, H., 1966. *The Rock Pictures of Europe*, Sidgwick & Jackson paperback.

Le Rouzic, Z., 1930. *Er Lannic*, Vannes.

Levy, G., 1963. *The Gate of Horn*, Faber paperback.

Mallery, G., 1888–9. *Picture-Writing of the American Indians*, 10th Annual Report of the Bureau of Ethnology to the Secretary of the Smithsonian Institution. Reprinted in 1972 by Dover Publications, New York. See Chapter V.

Matthews, W. H., 1922. *Mazes and Labyrinths*, Longmans.

Powell, T. G. E., 1960. *Megalithic and Other Art: Centre and West*, in *Ant* XXXIV p. 180–190.

Rivett-Carnac, J. H., 1879. *Notes on Ancient Sculpturings on Rocks . . . ,* J. Asiatic Soc Bengal reprint, Calcutta.

Savory, H. N., 1968. *Spain and Portugal*, Thames & Hudson, see p. 209–212.

Simpson, D. D. A., and Thawley, J. E., 1972. *Single Grave Art in Britain*, in *SAF* No 4, see p. 89 and p. 97–98.

Sobrino-Buhigas, R., 1935. *Corpus Petroglyphorum Gallaeciae*, text in Latin.

Valcamonica Symposium, 1970. *Actes du Symposium International d'Art Préhistorique*, Edizioni del Centro, Capo di Ponte.

Abbreviations

AA	Archaeologia Aeliana
Ant	Antiquity
Ant Jnl	Antiquaries' Journal
Archaeol	Archaeologia, Society of Antiquaries
Arch Cambr	Archaeologia Cambrensis
BNC	History of the Berwickshire Naturalists' Club
CA	Current Archaeology
JCHAS	Journal of the Cork Historical and Archaeological Society
JKAS	Journal of the Kilkenny Archaeological Society (later JRSAI)
JRSAI	Journal of the Royal Society of Antiquaries of Ireland
PPS	Proceedings of the Prehistoric Society
PRIA	Proceedings of the Royal Irish Academy
PSAS	Proceedings of the Society of Antiquaries of Scotland
SAF	Scottish Archaeological Forum
Tr Anc Mons Soc	Transactions of the Ancient Monuments Society
UJA	Ulster Journal of Archaeology
YAJ	Yorkshire Archaeological Journal

Sites to Visit

This is a selection of the more impressive and easily accessible carving sites in Britain. For sites in areas not visited by the author, see references under regional headings in 'List of Useful Works'.

NORTHERN ENGLAND

West Yorkshire—Ordnance Survey 1″ map 96

There are two useful maps plotting cup-and-ring stones at Ilkley and Baildon in B. M. Marsden's *Discovering Regional Archaeology, NW England* (Shire publications 1971) although the more remote sites are hard to find.

Ilkley Moor   Some of the best stones are within a short walk from the streets of the town. The fragments of the Panorama Stone are preserved within railings opposite St Margaret's Church (SE 115473). The upper road to Heber's Ghyll leads to the area where these rocks were originally situated, and if the visitor continues on the path beside the reservoir the Swastika Stone on Woodhouse Crag (094470) is eventually reached, also enclosed by railings. The most spectacular carvings are on the Hanging Stones (128467) which can be reached by a steep path from the cattle grid on the upper road at the outskirts of town about $\frac{1}{4}$ mile before it climbs up to the Cow and Calf Hotel.

Baildon Moor, accessible from Bingley or Shipley. The major group of stones are inconspicuously sited on top of the hill near the N. wall of Dobrudden Farm caravan park. See also the large stone, sometimes turf-covered, just S.E. of the Farm (SE 400138).

Snowden Moor   The sketch map in Cowling 1936–8 is a little misleading, especially as the scale is wrong. The only major carving which the author can now find on Snowden Carr is the Tree of Life stone (SE 180511). This can be reached by an old field wall leading W. from the minor road about $\frac{1}{2}$ mile N. from the crossroads on the moor. The visitor should follow the wall up the hill. The stone is a little beyond the corner on the left-hand side of the path.

Northumberland—O. S. 1″ map 71

The references listed under M. H. Dodds are useful for the visitor, and see Hogg 1956 for a large scale map of the Doddington Moor stones. The sites are here described working south towards Rothbury.

Roughting Linn NT 984367. This great rock is situated just W. of the minor road between Milfield and Lowick beside an Iron Age fort.

Dod Law The major concentration in Northumberland lies on high ground to the E. and S. E. of Doddington. Several interesting stones can be found in and around the remains of two Iron Age forts overlooking the River Till by the Shepherd's House. The major slab decorated with irregular squares and other patterns lies on level ground between the two camps and behind the house (NU 005317).

Chatton Law NU 073294. A series of carvings, including a deep channel some 30 feet long, near the Iron Age hillfort accessible from road about one mile E. of Chatton.

Weetwood Moor/Whitsunbank Two impressive rocks can be found without much difficulty, one with a channel (NU 010280) on the edge of a gentle slope facing Coldmartin Lough to S.E., the other among a series of outcrops just N. of gate between Weetwood and Fowberry beside moor road (022282).

Fowberry Park NU 030277. See Gunn 1885–6. On the edge of an old quarry between Fowberry Mains and Fowberry Park, not far from stone wall. Cups and rings and two unusual carvings, one with rectangle of midget cups.

Old Bewick NU 078216. The first cup-and-ring group to be 'discovered' in the last century lies near an Iron Age fort accessible from footpath off Alnwick–Wooler road.

Morwick NU 233044. See Dodds 1899. Outcrop on S. side of River Coquet with carvings on vertical faces, of uncertain date. Reach by awkward path along river bank from ford at 236050.

Lordenshaws NU 056994. See Newbigin 1932. Spectacular cups and rings, basins and channels lie on the western and eastern slopes below a very well-preserved hillfort.

SCOTLAND

The South-West—Galloway—O. S. 1″ maps 80–81
See Morris 1964–6 and 1966–7.

Cardroness House, Anwoth, Kirkcudbright, NX 566535. In private garden are three very fine stones moved from nearby sites.

Cauldside Burn, Kirkcudbright, NX 529575. Remarkable spiral on block across the burn N. from the main cairn and stone circle in the valley N. of Cairnharrow Hill. Approach by minor roads and old military road from A75.

Broughton Mains, Wigtown NX 457457, a site fenced by DOE a short distance W. of road 4 miles N. of Whithorn.

Drumtroddan, Wigtown, NX 362444, a fine set of carvings fenced in a field on Drumtroddan Farm off A714 about a mile E. of Port William.

Knock   A spiral on a small rock near top of hillock overlooking the sea. Reach by minor road S.W. off A747 and gap in wall 75 yards beyond cattle grid. Hillock is same distance W.S.W. (NX 364402).

Argyll—O. S. 1″ map 52.
See Campbell and Sandeman 1961–2 and Scott 1966.

Ormaig NM 821028. Outcrop on slope facing S.W. Most easily accessible by boat hire from Ardfern.

Torran NR 879049. Cup-marked and cross-inscribed standing stone on the left of the road about a mile N. of Ford crossroads.

Kilmartin Valley   The extensive prehistoric remains, all well-preserved and signposted, include decorated cist stones in cairns of the linear cemetery to S.W. of Kilmartin. See Nether Largie N. Cairn (NR 832985) with trapdoor access to central cist, Nether Largie Mid-Cairn (next in line to S.S.W., 831983) with side cist and axe (?) carvings, and Ri Cruin ($\frac{1}{2}$ mile to S.S.W., 825972) with S. cist and axe carvings, 'ship' slab now in National Museum, Edinburgh. The cup-marked standing stone monuments at Kilmartin, near the line of the cemetery at 828977 and at Ballymeanoch, to W. of A816 at 834964, should not be missed. The signposted stone circle at Temple Wood (826979) includes spiral carving at base of due N. stone when seen from central cist.

Poltalloch NR 812963. A fine rock partially turf-covered and in a sloping position just below farm road on private Poltalloch estate.

Kilmichael Glassary NR 858934. Signposted and fenced rock in village overlooking church.

Torbhlaran NR 864945. Cup-marked standing stone beside road about one mile N. of Kilmichael Glassary. To S.W. are two whale-backed outcrops with cups and rings.

Cairnbaan NR 838910. Two enclosed and signposted rocks on high ground reached by path behind Cairnbaan Hotel, which is situated beside bridge over Crinan Canal.

Barnakill NR 82199155. Pair of hands carved on a boulder forming part of a ruined dyke. It is very difficult to find. A track leads from N. side of Crinan Canal by lock-keeper's cottage. The rock is east of the track and N.W. of a small walled conifer plantation.

Achnabreck NR 856906. Britain's largest carving site. Reach via Achnabreck Farm road E. of A816 about a mile N. of Lochgilphead. Signs point the way from the farmhouse.

IRELAND

Peter Harbison's paperback *Guide to the National Monuments of Ireland* (Gill and Macmillan 1970) is useful and entertaining. Ordnance survey maps are readily obtainable only at the $\frac{1}{2}$-inch scale, but for general location of sites this presents few problems for the cup-and-ring hunter.

Meath—O. S. $\frac{1}{2}''$ map 13

Newgrange 0/007727. The Boyne tombs lie off minor roads S. of T26 Slane–Drogheda, about 5 miles from Slane. There are conducted tours of the Newgrange passage and chamber, and there is an information centre nearby.

Knowth N/990730. Beside minor road between Newgrange and Slane. The site will remain closed to the public for some years while excavations and restorations continue.

Dowth 0/020740. Just over a mile from Newgrange towards Drogheda to S. of road. A few kerbstones on the E. side of the mound are exposed, including stone with multiple 'sun' motifs. The key to the two passage graves can be obtained from Miss Rose Hoey at Knowth but it is arguable whether the dank and crampt conditions of the main tomb make the effort worthwhile.

Tara N/920600, W. of the Dublin–Navan road about 7 miles S. of Navan. On top of the hill, surrounded by earthworks of many periods, is the prominent Mound of the Hostages. The chamber is kept locked although the decorated stone is visible.

Fourknocks 0/110620. Just N. of road through Fourknocks village about 2 miles N.W. of Naul. The key is available from Mr T. Conwell at first house on left from stile. Perhaps the next most impressive tomb after Newgrange.

Loughcrew cemetery N/570-600.770-780. A minor road off the L3 Crossakeel–Oldcastle leads to lay-by between the two major hilltop concentrations of passage graves, Cairnbane West and East. The map reproduced in Harbison 1970, p. 188, and elsewhere, is useful for finding sites. Cairns T and L are usually locked, although ruined graves especially on Cairnbane West have easily accessible oranmented stones.

Cork—O. S. $\frac{1}{2}''$ map 24

Drumbeg W/247352. The best known stone circle in Co. Cork, sign-posted off L191 between Glandore and Ross Carbery. The upper surface of the recumbent stone is ornamented with cups and a grooved outline, perhaps representing an axe.

Kerry—O. S. $\frac{1}{2}''$ map 20.

Note: the Gortboy stone described in several sources has recently been destroyed.

Temple Feaghna bullaun stone V/966641. Take narrow E. road off T65 a mile N. of Beaurearagh river. Turn left at a T-junction, and then right over the next bridge one mile further on. The stone is on the left of the road $\frac{1}{2}$ mile further on.

Poulacapple V/847723. Take the minor road to Ruscussane off the T66 about 4 miles W. of Kenmare. A peculiarly carved stone lies near left-hand side of road below the house of Mrs Downing just beyond Bay View Farm.

Staigue Bridge V/611633 (sheet 24). This extensive pattern of cups and rings is located near one of Ireland's most imposing prehistoric stone forts, well-signposted N. off the T66. About $\frac{1}{2}$ mile S. of Staigue, the road bends to the W. and runs beside a disused bridge. From this bridge, about 100 yards to the E., the large outcrop is clearly visible.

Coolnaharagill Upper/Mountain Stage V/624884. Mrs Jackson of the Mountain Stage guest house (signposted S. just off the Glenbeigh–Kells road) has built a garden alcove around a boulder with concentric circles.

Lake Coomasaharn. See O'Kelly 1958. An impressive group of cup-and-ring stones on farmland owned by Mr J. P. Quirke, near the final right angle bend of a tarred minor road which leads from the T66 at Glenbeigh to the head of Lake Coomasaharn. The carvings are in boulder-strewn fields and are almost impossible to find without local help which is readily given. V/632852.

Derrynablaha. See Anati 1963. At least two dozen carvings are known from the rocky slopes around Mr D. O'Sullivan's farm which faces eastwards towards Lough Brin, some 2 miles S. of the Ballaghbeama Gap. A few hundred yards S. of the farm the road bends to the E. across a stream, which should be followed on foot up the steep slope to the S.W. until the table-like Rock 10 is reached. Rock 12 is on the slopes below this spot but it is difficult to find. V/765775.

Gates of Glory Q/429010. A massive cup-and-ring boulder, apparently lying on top of a small cairn, is in a field near the standing stones known as the Gates of Glory. The stones are just N. off the Dingle–Ventry road, $\frac{1}{2}$ mile W. of Milltown opposite a cemetery.

Index of Names